# WHAT TO FEED
## YOUR
## ❖ BABY ❖

# WHAT TO FEED
# YOUR
# BABY

## How to give your baby the best of health and vitality

*With over 50 fantastic step-by-step recipes for every stage of development*

## SARA LEWIS

SMITHMARK

This edition published in 1996 by
SMITHMARK Publishers
a division of U.S. Media Holdings, Inc.
16 East 32nd Street
New York, NY 10016.

SMITHMARK books are available for bulk purchase
for sales and promotion and premium use. For details
write or call the manager of special sales,
SMITHMARK Publishers, 16 East 32nd Street,
New York, NY 10016; (212) 532–6600.

ISBN 0–8317–7180–1

Produced by Anness Publishing Limited
1 Boundary Row
London SE1 8HP

This book was previously published as part of a larger
compendium, *Cooking for Babies and Toddlers*

Typeset by MC Typeset Ltd
Printed in Singapore by Star Standard Industries Pte. Ltd.

Publisher: Joanna Lorenz
Project Editors: Judith Simons and Emma Wish
Designer: Sue Storey
Special Photography: John Freeman
Stylist: Judy Williams
Home Economists: Sara Lewis, Jacqueline Clarke
and Petra Jackson

10 9 8 7 6 5 4 3 2 1

# CONTENTS

# INTRODUCTION

Introducing your baby to the delights of solid food heralds the beginning of a new and exciting stage in your baby's development. Although it will be a few months yet before your baby will be able to share in family meals fully, the foods that you give your baby now are vitally important not only for their nutritional benefits but also in laying down the first foundations for a healthy diet through childhood and beyond. There are several important factors to consider when planning your baby's diet: at what stage to begin weaning; what foods to serve and when; and how to prepare foods quickly and easily while still providing the nutrient-dense diet babies need to support their rapid growth. Your baby's progression from milk feedings to solids will be gradual. Start with rice cereal which is barely warm and only slightly thicker than milk, before moving on to those first few spoonfuls of smooth puréed vegetables and fruit. Then, stage by stage, you will be able to introduce your baby to a tempting array of new flavors and textures.

# FIRST FOODS

Although during the first few years of any baby's life, food, diet and nutrition are vitally important – to build a healthy and energetic child and to develop good eating habits that will see the infant safely through childhood – there is a real shortage of reliable, practical information on the subject.

This book aims to outline all you need to know about feeding your baby. The book is packed with over 50 healthy recipes, all beautifully illustrated with color pictures – from first purées, to finger foods and introducing those first tempting toddler meals.

In the very early days all a baby needs is milk, but as it grows so too will its nutritional needs. By four months most babies will have doubled their birth weight and will be ready to begin mini-mouthfuls of smooth purée.

Although this marks an exciting time in your baby's development it can also cause immense worry for a new parent. We all want to provide the best for our child and what better start in life than to begin laying the foundations for a healthy diet? But what do you do if your child won't eat, or just spits out those delicious spoonfuls of food that you have so lovingly prepared?

If your child has any food allergies or sensitivities read each recipe carefully to make sure it doesn't contain a problem ingredient.

## FIRST FOODS

This book covers everything you need to know about introducing those first few spoonfuls of smooth puréed foods: including when to begin weaning, the signs to look out for, what foods to serve and when, basic equipment, plus sound

nutritional advice, helpful guidelines on food preparation and tons of colorful and exciting recipes to tempt your baby. Babies who are on soy formula because of an allergy to milk can be fed the purées described in this section prepared with soy formula instead of milk.

You will almost certainly find that helpful friends, relatives, health

Above: *Mediterranean Vegetable Mash is just one of the many delicious recipes to discover in this book.*

professionals and magazines will offer you sometimes useful and occasionally inappropriate advice. This book draws on current dietary information to provide the most up-to-date advice available.

## FOOD AND YOUR BABY

Childrens' nutritional needs are very different from our own. Forget about low fat, high fiber diets. Young children require nutrient-dense foods to meet their rapid levels of growth. Requirements for protein and energy are high in proportion to the child's size. Tiny tummies mean children are unable to eat large quantities of food while at the same time they are usually very active. Their appetites can vary enormously, but the range of foods that they will eat may also be very limited. So it is vital that the foods which are eaten contain a variety of nutrients, in combination with calories, while still fitting in with family meals. High fiber foods can be very filling without providing sufficient levels of protein, vitamins and minerals.

For young children fat is the major source of dietary calories: both breastmilk and infant formula contribute about 50% of calories as fat. As your child progresses to a mixed diet, the proportion of calories supplied by fat decreases and is replaced by carbohydrates. But it is important that the calories are provided by fat up to the age of two, as too many carbohydrates may be too bulky for a young child.

Adequate calories are necessary to sustain growth. Fat is a very useful source of calories and the main source of the fat soluble vitamins, A, D, E and K, while also providing essential fatty acids that the body cannot make itself. It is best to obtain fat from foods which contain other essential nutrients: whole milk, cheese, yogurts, lean meat and small quantities of oily fish.

Try to include a portion of carbohydrates in every meal once your child is over nine months: for example bread, potatoes, rice or pasta. Encourage young children to eat a variety of fruits and vegetables.

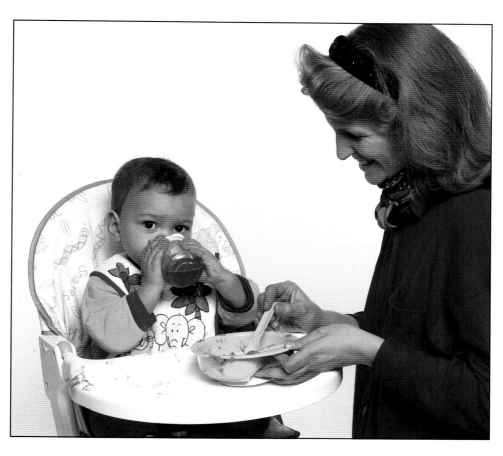

As with adults, try to keep salt intake to a minimum, and omit it altogether from home-prepared baby meals. Fried foods or very sugary foods should also be generally discouraged.

Obviously eating a healthy, well-balanced diet is essential for any age group, but social skills are also important. Our children learn from us and so it is also vital to eat together as a family, if not every day, then as often as possible, so that young children can discover not only how to behave at the table but also that eating is a sociable and enjoyable experience.

We do hope this book will make mealtimes fun for the entire family and help to minimize any problems and anxieties you may come up against when feeding your baby.

Right: *Babies are easily encouraged to take pleasure in their food, especially if they are able to help themselves!*

Above: *Start with simple vegetable purées at around four months.*

# Weaning to Solids

Most babies are ready to begin those first few mini-mouthfuls of puréed foods at around four months and almost all babies will be eating solid food by six months. By this age babies need the extra energy, protein, iron and other essential nutrients that are found in solids in order to help them develop and grow. Your baby will also be progressing from sucking to biting and chewing – as many breast-feeding mothers find out!

Remember that every baby has individual needs, so don't be surprised if your baby seems ready for solids earlier or later than other babies of the same age. Don't feel pressured by friends with young babies, or helpful relatives. Be guided by your own baby.

**WHAT TO LOOK OUT FOR**
- if your baby still seems hungry after nursing
- wants feeding more frequently
- starts waking at night after some weeks of sleeping through
- shows a real interest in the foods that you are eating
- seems more restless

If your baby is showing some or all of these signs then she is probably ready to begin solids. Check with your pediatrician; a few large and very hungry babies may show these signs earlier than four months, but the majority of babies should not be given solid foods before four months as their digestive systems can't cope.

Be guided as well by any family history of allergies, eczema or asthma. Studies suggest that babies who are fed on breast milk or formula somewhat longer are less likely to develop these complaints.

In the early days of weaning, your baby is not dependent on solid food

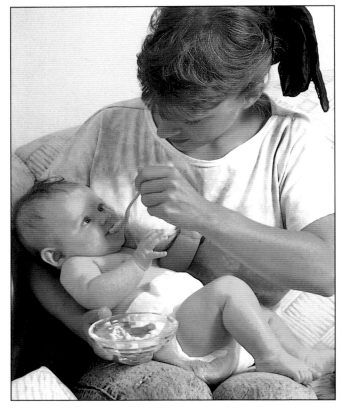

Left: *When the signs are right, start your baby with a few mouthfuls of puréed food. Your baby will feel most comfortable seated on your lap at this stage, and adopting one of the positions you have used for breast feeding will enhance security and confidence.*

Below: *If you have any doubts or worries about the right time to try purées and solids, your pediatrician will be able to help.*

Above: *Your baby will very quickly take an interest in your hand and the spoon, and will play as she eats.*

for the supply of nutrients as this is still met by milk or formula. Don't worry if she only takes a taste of food – the actual experience of taking food off a spoon is the important thing. However, by six months the baby's body store of nutrients has been used up and solid foods are crucial for supplying all the vital minerals and vitamins your baby needs.

## WHAT ABOUT NURSING?

During the early stages of weaning, solids are given in addition to the normal feedings of breast milk or formula. As mixed feeding continues your baby will naturally cut down on the number of milk feedings, although milk will remain an important part of a child's diet.

Up to six months your baby should be having at least four milk feedings a day and by age one your baby needs at least 1 pint whole milk a day. Milk will still be contributing 40 percent of the energy she uses up.

More and more health professionals are now recommending that children should not be given cows' milk as their main drink until after 12 months, due to low levels of iron and vitamins C and D. Mothers are sometimes advised to go on to fortified formula when breastfeeding has finished. Small amounts of cows'

Above: *Bottles are a wonderful aid, but try to wean your baby off them by age one, or the sucking habit can be difficult to break.*

Above: *Every baby is different. There is no need to be worried if your baby seems ready for solids earlier or later than other babies.*

milk may be used in cooking from six months, but it is better to use formula.

Whole cows' milk can be given to children between one and two, while part-skim milk can be gradually introduced to those over two providing the child eats well. Skim milk should not be given to children under five.

Only give pasteurized milk to children. Long-life milk is a useful standby for holidays and traveling as it doesn't need to be refrigerated, although once opened treat as whole pasteurized milk.

Some people prefer to give goats' or sheeps' milk feeling it is less allergenic and offers additional nourishment, although this cannot be substantiated. Goats' milk is deficient in folic acid and must not be given to babies under six months. Boil goats' milk before use, as it may be sold unpasteurized.

## WEANING FROM BREAST OR BOTTLE

You can go on breastfeeding your baby, as well as giving solid food, for as long as you wish. But many mothers are quite relieved when their baby is happy to try a feeder

cup or bottle along with their lunchtime "solid" meal.

Once solids become established the number of daytime milk feedings naturally decreases with just the special morning and evening comfort feedings continuing until you and baby are ready to stop.

Whether bottle or breast and bottle feeding, try to wean your baby off the bottle completely by the age of one. Otherwise your baby may find it difficult to give the bottle up and comfort sucking on a nipple can be a hard habit to break.

Once your baby can sit up and is settled into three meals a day then you can introduce a lidded feeding cup – initially at one meal a day, then at two and so on. But do make sure to cuddle your baby while giving a drink so that the baby still enjoys the closeness and security of being with mother or father. There may be a few setbacks when your baby is teething or unwell, but be guided by your baby.

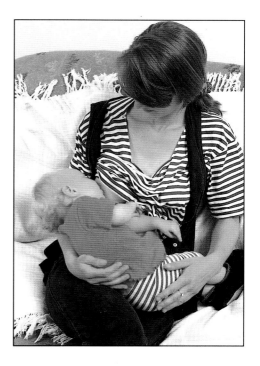

Above: *It won't all happen at once: a mixed period of feeding with breast, bottle and simple solids is perfectly natural and healthy.*

# Introducing Solid Food

Many parents find that around late morning, after their baby's morning nap, is the best time to introduce solids. Baby is happy and nicely hungry without being frantic. Offer a small milk feeding to take the edge off her immediate hunger and make her feel secure, and then go on to offer solid food. Finish with the rest of the milk feeding or "second side."

## SITTING COMFORTABLY

In the early days sit baby on your lap, protect her with a bib and yourself with a dish towel and hold the baby tightly so she feels secure. As you and baby become more confident about feeding then you may prefer to strap her into a portable car seat or baby chair. Most babies will be unable to sit in a highchair until six months or so.

## FIRST SPOONFULS

First foods should be very smooth and mild in taste. Rice cereal is often the most successful because its milky taste and soft texture seem vaguely familiar to the baby. Begin by trying a teaspoonful of rice cereal, add a little previously boiled water, expressed breast milk or formula as the package directs, and mix to make a smooth runny purée, slightly thicker than milk. Test the

Above: *First rice cereal will be barely warm, and only very slightly thicker than milk.*

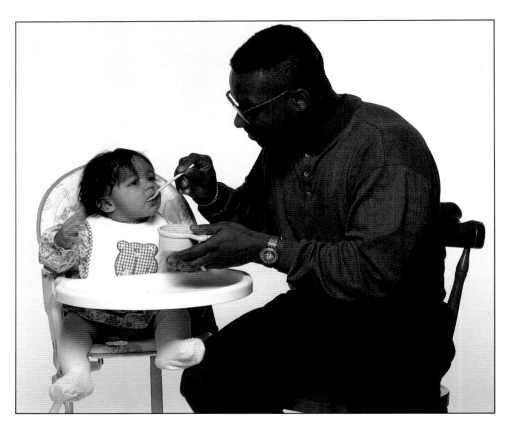

Above: *At about six months your baby will be ready to sit safely in a highchair. You should always use a strap.*

Left: *A good interim stage between lap feeding and the highchair is a baby chair on the floor, or even a portable car seat.*

temperature on the edge of your lip; it should be just lukewarm – too hot and you may put baby off solids completely. Offer tiny amounts on the end of a sterilized teaspoon. Learning to eat from a spoon is quite a skill and your baby may start by spitting out the food until she has mastered the technique of taking food off the spoon and transferring it to the back of her mouth. Go at your baby's pace and don't try to hurry things. If your baby seems reluctant, then abandon the feeding and go back to breast or bottle feeding. You could try solids again a few days later – there's plenty of time. Never force-feed and never add solid foods to a baby's bottle as it can lead to choking which can be dangerous.

Once your baby has accepted the idea of eating from a spoon continue with a midday meal of rice cereal or

## SPOON FEEDING FOR THE FIRST TIME

**1** Sit your baby on your lap in a familiar position. Always test the temperature of the food.

**2** Offer the spoon to your baby. Go slowly and if the spoon or food is rejected try again another day.

**3** When your baby has taken its first solid food, sit quietly for a little while in an upright position.

puréed potato for a week or two to give her digestive system a chance to adjust to the new food.

After that, you could gradually introduce puréed carrot, parsnip and rutabaga, or applesauce or puréed pears. As always be guided by your baby: this is a slow process so don't try to hurry your baby if she is not ready or you will run the risk of putting her off altogether.

After three to four weeks your baby may be ready to try two mini meals a day. Increase the amount of food to 2 tsp, even 3 tsp at each meal if your baby seems ready. You may be able to slightly reduce the amount of formula or breast milk you use to make the purée so that it is not quite so liquid.

If your baby likes the flavor, then offer it again for a few meals before introducing a new taste. If your baby spits out the food with obvious distaste then go back to rice cereal or try mixing the new flavor with a little rice cereal so that it is milder and more palatable.

Try to follow your baby's appetite and pace; most babies will stop when they have had enough. Don't be tempted to persuade your baby to finish off those last few spoonfuls.

It's a bad habit to make or encourage anyone to clear the plate if they are full. If you do it with a baby, she'll probably be sick!

Adopt a feeding schedule to suit you both. In the early days it may be easier to give baby breakfast before older children get up, or after they're at school, when the house is quieter.

Six to eight weeks into solid feeding and your baby will probably be ready for three small meals a day. But again be guided by her needs and appetite, so don't introduce a third meal until you feel she is really ready. Aim to feed your baby at roughly equal time intervals that will eventually coincide with as many family meals as possible.

TIPS
- Be guided by your baby and your pediatrician.
- Sterilize all equipment before use.
- Don't force your baby if she doesn't seem ready for solids.
- Maintain milk feedings and offer plain boiled water or very diluted fruit juice as well.
- Try one taste at a time and continue with this until your baby is accustomed to it. If she doesn't like it, don't offer it for a few days.
- Remember, babies don't mind repetition, they've been living on milk for months!

Above: *Over the weeks you can build up the diet from rice cereal to items like puréed carrot, parsnip, apple or pear, gradually leaving more texture as your baby seems ready.*

## EQUIPMENT

Choose a small plastic spoon, preferably with a shallow bowl that is gentle on your baby's gums. Look out for packs of weaning spoons in pharmacies or baby-care shops. If you don't want to buy a lot of equipment right away you may find it useful to mix small quantities of rice cereal in the sterilized cap of a bottle. Alternatively, use a small china ramekin or plastic bowl. Plastic bowls with suction feet or stay-warm linings are also perfectly adequate and will be useful later on when baby gets bigger. All equipment must be sterilized first and water must be previously boiled and cooled before use.

Below: *This dish and the spoon with the shallow bowl would be the perfect starter set.*

Top left, above, left and below: *Any small dish, or even the lid off a baby bottle, can be used for mixing and feeding so long as it is thoroughly sterilized.*

Below: *Bib*

Left: *Bowl with stay-warm lining.*

Below: *Your baby will graduate from bottles with nipples to cups and beakers with tight-fitting lids. There is a variety of types, but you will find one the toddler likes.*

## FEEDING TWINS

Probably the easiest way is to sit each child in their car or baby seat, side by side, and offer food from one bowl. Twins can get rather frustrated if you have to keep picking up different bowls and spoons. Try to be adaptable and if you find a way that works then stick with it. Encourage finger foods slightly earlier: perhaps a tiny ham sandwich, or cooked broccoli floret or carrot stick.

Wait until each child has finished their main course before offering dessert as the slow eater will be distracted and want to go on to dessert too.

Caring for twins can be exhausting so you may find serving sandwiches for lunch an easier option and this will give you a chance to eat something too. Serve a cooked main meal for dinner.

## DRINKS

Although your baby will need less milk for nourishment, she will still need something to drink, especially in hot weather. Always offer at least two drinks during the day along with a drink with every meal.

### You can give:
● milk – breast milk, formula or, at over one year, whole cows' milk
● cooled boiled water
● well-diluted pure unsweetened fruit juice.

Above: *Dilute juices with boiled water.*

You can stop boiling the water for baby's drinks when you stop sterilizing her feeding equipment, but always make sure you allow the tap to run for a while before using. Never use water from the hot tap for drinks.

If you have a water softener make sure that you use a tap connected directly to the main water supply and independent of the water softener. Artificially softened water is not recommended as salts are added during the softening process. Check with your pediatrician before giving a baby bottled water as the mineral content varies and you will need to choose a low-mineral brand such as those labeled "spring water." As a general rule, bottled water is not really necessary unless you are vacationing somewhere where it is unsafe to drink the water.

Some fruit drinks contain a lot of added sugar, so check the label for sucrose, glucose, dextrose, fructose, maltose, syrup, honey or concentrated fruit juice. If you do give concentrated drinks to your baby make sure you dilute them correctly and do not give them too often. Pure fruit juices contain no

Above: *Feed twins side by side, alternating servings between the two.*
Below: *Drinks fill up the baby's tummy – so offer drinks after food.*

added sugar. At first, dilute them one part juice to three parts water. The amount of water can be reduced as the child matures. Offer drinks at the end of meal times once your baby is settled into three meals a day.

Never allow a baby to use a bottle of juice as a comforter or go to sleep with a bottle in his mouth as this can result in serious tooth decay.

# Food Preparation

At this first stage it is vital that whatever solid food you offer should be smooth and soft in texture. Puréeing foods is very simple and there are plenty of gadgets available to make it even easier. For ease and speed, an electric blender is by far the best. You may be able to buy a blender attachment for your mixer or look out for a freestanding blender unit. Prices vary considerably so it's worth shopping around. A food processor works well, but make sure the food is blended to a very fine purée before offering it to your baby, since processors can miss the odd lump, especially when processing small quantities. A hand-held electric multimixer is another useful gadget with the bonus of reducing washing up by mixing foods directly in the serving bowl. If you prefer to purée food by hand, then a strainer or hand mill are both perfectly adequate and are much cheaper alternatives.

Above: *There is a huge range of brand-name food processors and blenders on the market, many of which have attachments for puréeing.*

Left: *The basics – manual mashers, or a strainer – take longer but will do the job just as well.*

Above: *A blender will make perfect purée in seconds. This is the right tool for making large batches.*

Above: *This hand-held blender takes a little longer, but the results are just as reliable. They are easy to clean and store.*

Above: *Making purée manually the old-fashioned way – with strainer and spoon – is time-consuming but highly satisfying.*

## FOOD HYGIENE

Young babies can easily pick up infections so it is vitally important that all equipment be scrupulously cleaned before use.

- Always wash your hands before handling food or feeding equipment.

Above: *Rule one – always wash your hands before feeding your baby or handling food.*

- All items such as bottles and containers used for freezing or storing baby food, feeding spoons and serving bowls should be sterilized in the usual way, by boiling in a saucepan of water for 25 minutes, or by using a steam sterilizer. Larger items such as a strainer, knife, saucepan, blender or masher or plastic chopping board should be scalded with boiling water.

Above: *Scald larger objects with boiling water to sterilize.*

Right: *Always keep the surfaces around where your baby eats scrupulously clean.*

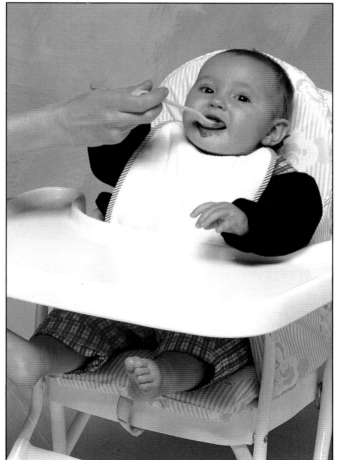

Above: *There is a wide range of sterilizing equipment to choose from. This group, all specially designed for bottles and nipples, comprises two steam sterilizing units that operate electrically and a traditional container (see right) that holds the bottles efficiently in cold water sterilizing solution.*

## SOLUTION STERILIZER

1 Fill the sterilizer to the required height with cold water, and add sterilizing tablets or liquid.

2 Pack the items to be sterilized into the container. Bottles will fit into the spaces provided.

3 Make sure no air gets trapped in the container – or these pockets will not be properly sterile. Push everything down with the "float."

4 Place the lid on and leave for the length of time specified in the instructions. Rinse everything afterwards in boiling water.

## STEAM STERILIZER

1 Measure the specified amount of water into the base of the steamer as directed in the manufacturer's instructions.

2 Pack the bottles and nipples into the container: steamers have less capacity for dishes or bowls, which will need to be boiled separately.

● Sterilize all baby equipment until she is six months; milk bottles, nipples etc. should be sterilized until she goes on to a cup.

Above: *Boiling in water for 25 minutes is still the simplest method of sterilizing.*

● Never use equipment used for the family pet when preparing baby food. Keep a can opener, fork and dish specifically for your pet and make sure other members of the family are aware of this.
● Once cooked, cover all baby food with a lid or plate and transfer to the refrigerator as soon as possible. Food should not be left for longer than 1½ hours at room temperature before refrigerating or freezing.

Above: *Always cover baby food at all times – even when stored in the refrigerator.*

## STERILIZING IN THE MICROWAVE

Microwave ovens are not suitable for general day-to-day sterilizing without special equipment, and many health authorities and mother and baby experts specifically recommend against using the microwave for this purpose.

However microwave sterilizing units can be purchased for sterilizing bottles, and where used, the manufacturer's instructions should be followed closely.

*Right: This sterilizing unit is specially made for microwave use.*

## BATCH COOKING

Cooking for a tiny baby can be very frustrating. Those tiny spoonfuls of super-smooth purée so lovingly and hygienically prepared, offered with such hope and spat out so unceremoniously can leave you feeling quite indignant.

Save time by cooking several meals in advance. Freeze mini portions in ice-cube trays, great for those early days when you need only one cube for lunch and flexible enough for later weeks when your baby's appetite has grown to two or three cubes per meal.

Spoon the mixture into sterilized ice-cube trays and freeze until solid. Press the cubes into a plastic bag or container, seal, label and return to the freezer. Keep batches of food in the same bag so flavors don't get mixed.

Recycle yogurt containers, cottage cheese containers with lids, small plastic containers with lids or use disposable plastic cups and cover with plastic wrap. Sterilize using sterilizing fluid or tablets. Cover all prepared foods and label clearly so you know what they are and when they went into the freezer.

Most foods should be used within three months if stored in a freezer at 0°F. Defrost plastic containers in the refrigerator overnight. Ice cubes can be left to defrost at room temperature in a bowl or on a plate, loosely covered with plastic wrap.

## BATCH COOKING TIPS

**1** It is just as quick (and very much cheaper in the long run) to make a larger batch of purée as a smaller quantity for a single meal.

**2** Freeze in meal-sized portions in sterilized ice-cube trays: these can later be turned out into freezer bags for storing.

**3** Make sure the bags are carefully labeled and dated. Keep only for the period specified in your freezer handbook.

# STAGE 1: FIRST TASTES – AROUND FOUR MONTHS

THE FIRST SOLIDS ARE A STEPPING-STONE TO INTRODUCING YOUR BABY TO REAL FOOD SO SHE BECOMES FAMILIAR WITH ALL SORTS OF DIFFERENT TASTES AND TEXTURES.

ALTHOUGH MILK IS STILL PROVIDING YOUR BABY WITH ALL HER NUTRITIONAL NEEDS THESE EARLY FOODS WILL BE THE GROUNDS ON WHICH LATER EATING HABITS ARE BUILT, SO IT IS IMPORTANT THAT THIS IS A HAPPY, POSITIVE EXPERIENCE. IT IS IMPORTANT TO BUILD ON GOOD FOUNDATIONS.

BEGIN BY OFFERING ONLY A TEASPOONFUL OF VERY SOFT RUNNY PURÉE ONCE A DAY, GRADUALLY BUILDING TO 2–3 TSP AND THEN SLOWLY ON TO TWO AND THREE MEALS A DAY.

## Suitable Foods

### FOODS TO INCLUDE

● rice cereal mixed with water, breast milk or formula.
● mild-tasting vegetable purées – beginning with potato then carrot, parsnip, or rutabaga purée.
● mild, naturally sweet fruit purées made with apples or pears.

**Apple**

**Pear**

**Rutabaga**

**Carrot**

**Potato**

**Parsnip**

**Rutabaga purée**

**Parsnip purée**

**Carrot purée**

**Potato purée**

**Pear purée**

**Applesauce**

**Rice cereal**

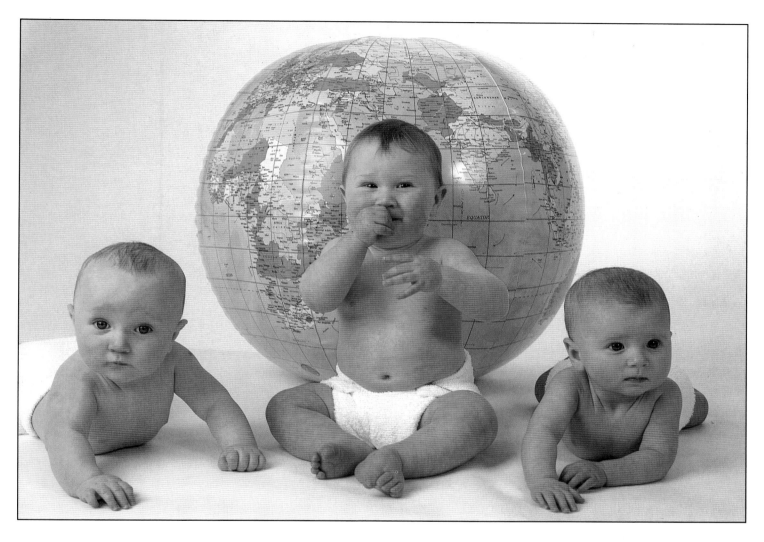

## FOODS TO AVOID
- highly spiced foods
- salt as this causes the kidneys to overwork. Avoid seasoning with salt or adding bouillon cubes, bacon and salami to foods
- cows' milk (give breast milk or formula feedings instead)
- foods containing gluten found in wheat, oats, rye and barley (check package labels)
- eggs
- meat, fish, poultry
- citrus fruits – can result in allergic reactions in some babies
- nuts, either whole or ground
- honey
- fatty foods

Right: *Adult favorites – but these must be avoided at this age, even as treats.*

Note: If you have a family history of allergies, your doctor may also advise you to avoid other foods as well. Do check with him.

Above: *A world of foodstuffs opens up over the months: but introduce them gradually, and at the right time.*

# Baby Rice

Mix 1–3 tsp rice cereal with cooled boiled water, breast milk or formula as the package directs. Cool slightly and test before serving.

Left: *Plain rice cereal will be the staple for your baby for the first few weeks of solids – then gradually add flavor and variation.*

# Vegetable Purées

**Makes: ¾ cup**

1 Peel 4oz potato, parsnip, carrot or rutabaga and dice.

2 Steam over a saucepan of boiling water for 10 minutes, until soft.

3 Press through a strainer, mix with 4–5 tbsp formula or breast milk depending on the vegetable used. Spoon a little into a bowl, test on a spoon and cool if needed. Cover the remaining purée and transfer to the refrigerator as soon as possible. Use within 24 hours.

● To microwave, put the vegetable or vegetables in a microwave-proof bowl with 2 tbsp formula or breast milk. Cover with plastic wrap, pierce and cook on High (100%) for 4 minutes. Let stand for 5 minutes, then press through a strainer and mix with 2–3 tbsp formula or breast milk. Cool and serve as described above.

Right: *This lovely selection of simple but satisfying vegetable purées illustrates that these bland foods need not lack color and variation, and can be made very attractive to the infant.*

# Fruit Purées

**Makes: ½ cup**

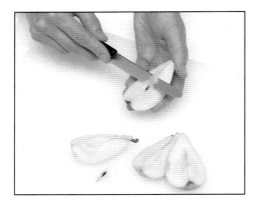

**1** Peel, quarter and core 1 eating apple or 1 ripe pear.

**2** Thinly slice and put in a small saucepan with 1 tbsp water, formula or breast milk. Cover and simmer for 10 minutes until soft.

● **To microwave:** place the apple or pear in a microwave-proof bowl with water, formula or breast milk. Cover with plastic wrap, pierce and cook on High (100%) for 3 minutes. Let stand for 5 minutes then press through a strainer. Cool and serve as above.

**3** Press through a strainer. Spoon a little purée into a serving bowl, test on a spoon and cool if needed. Cover, transfer to the refrigerator, and use within 24 hours.

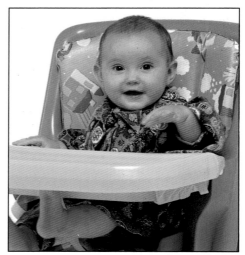

Top: *Pear (top) and apple purée will bring a smile to any baby's face (above).*

**Melon purée**

**Strawberry purée**

Left: *These tasty purées will encourage even reluctant eaters to take solids regularly.*

Warning: *Soft berry fruits should be introduced at around five to six months at the earliest. Do so in very small portions as some infants may have allergies and always strain the purée carefully to remove berry pips.*

Right: *When your baby is ready to start taking solids at around four to five months old, start with a teaspoon and build gradually to two and finally three meals a day.*

# STAGE 2: AROUND FIVE TO SIX MONTHS

B Y NOW YOUR BABY MAY BE TAKING SOLIDS AT TWO OR THREE MEALS EACH DAY. INCREASE THE VARIETY OF FOODS OFFERED AND START TO COMBINE FOOD TASTES. BABY PURÉE CAN BE A SLIGHTLY THICKER COARSER TEXTURE, BUT MAKE SURE THERE ARE NO PITS OR BONES. ALWAYS CHOOSE THE BEST, FRESHEST INGREDIENTS AND MAKE SURE UTENSILS ARE SCRUPULOUSLY CLEAN.

## *Suitable Foods*

### FOODS TO INCLUDE
- wider selection of vegetables including fresh or frozen peas, corn, cauliflower, broccoli, cabbage, spinach, celery, mushrooms, leeks
- poultry
- mild tasting fresh or frozen fish – sole, cod, haddock, trout
- small quantities of very lean red meat
- small quantities of split legumes – peas, red lentils and very well cooked or canned whole legumes – chickpeas, beans
- more interesting fruits – banana, apricots, peaches, plums, strawberries, raspberries, melon (Warning: offer tiny amounts of soft berry fruits as some children may be allergic to them.)
- gluten-free cereals – rice, cornstarch
- small quantities of cocoa

Celery

Mixed vegetables

Cabbage

Broccoli

Spinach

Corn

Chicken

Fish

Lean red meat

Plums

Banana

Apricots

Melon

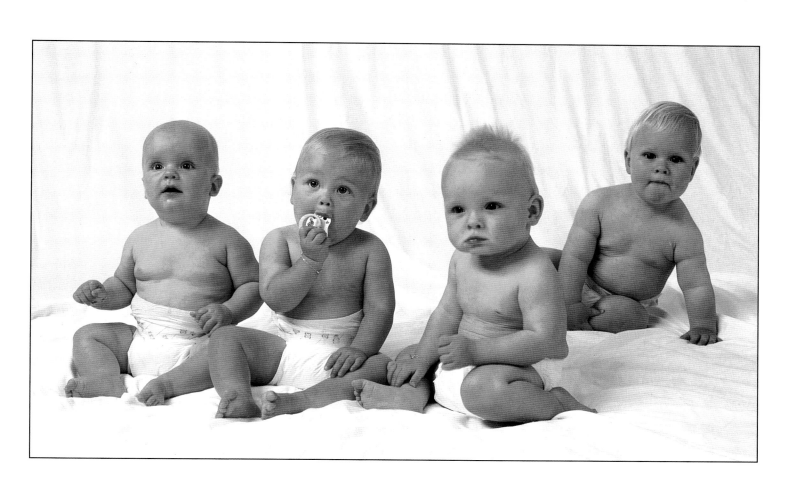

Above: *Every day brings a new taste: these young gourmets can't wait!*

**Chickpeas**

**Cocoa**

**Split peas**

**Cornstarch**

**Lentils**

**Rice**

**FOODS TO AVOID**
- gluten-based cereals, wheat flour and bread
- cows' milk and milk products
- eggs
- citrus fruit
- nuts, ground or whole
- fatty foods
- chilies and highly spiced foods

Below: *Even super-healthy adult foods such as whole wheat bread and oranges should still be avoided at this stage.*

# Reheating, Freezing and Using a Microwave

**REHEATING BABY FOOD**

Reheating food sounds straightforward but it is vitally important that these rules are followed as tepid food provides the perfect breeding ground for bacteria, especially if left uncovered in a warm kitchen and reheated several times.

● Don't reheat food more than once. It is a health risk.

● If you have a large batch of baby food then reheat just a portion in a saucepan and leave the remaining mixture in a covered bowl in the refrigerator. If your baby is still hungry then reheat a little extra again with the remaining mixture left in the refrigerator.

● Reheat small quantities of baby food in a sterilized heat-proof container, covered with a saucer or small plate and put into a small saucepan half filled with boiling water. Or spoon larger quantities straight into a saucepan, cover and bring to a boil.

● Make sure food is piping hot all the way through to kill any bacteria. Food should be 158°F for a minimum of 2 minutes. Remove from the heat and allow to cool. Test before serving to baby.

1 Reheat small quantities in a sterilized bowl, covered with a dish or aluminum foil.

2 Place the bowl into a pan half filled with boiling water. Make sure the food is cooked through.

3 For larger quantities, put the food straight into the pan and bring to a boil.

**FREEZING**

When using a freezer for storing homemade baby foods, use up the foods as soon as possible as the texture preferred by the child will change very quickly as the child develops.

Keeping a well-stocked freezer of basics can be a lifesaver: there is nothing worse than going shopping with little children, especially when they're tired, and freezing will save you trip after trip.

Make sure to always label foods so you know exactly when they went into the freezer and double check storage against this handy list of dates:

**Meat and poultry**

| | |
|---|---|
| Beef and lamb | 4–6 months |
| Pork and veal | 4–6 months |
| Ground beef | 3–4 months |
| Sausages and sausage meat | 2–3 months |
| Ham and bacon | 3–4 months |
| Chicken and turkey | 10–12 months |
| Duck and goose | 4–6 months |

**Fish**

| | |
|---|---|
| White fish | 6–8 months |
| Oily fish | 3–4 months |
| Fish portions | 3–4 months |
| Shellfish | 2–3 months |

**Fruit and vegetables**

| | |
|---|---|
| Fruit with or without sugar | 8–10 months |
| Fruit juices | 4–6 months |
| Most vegetables | 10–12 months |
| Mushrooms and tomatoes | 6–8 months |

**Dairy produce**

| | |
|---|---|
| Cream | 6–8 months |
| Butter, unsalted | 6–8 months |
| Butter, salted | 3–4 months |
| Cheese, hard | 4–6 months |
| Cheese, soft | 3–4 months |
| Ice cream | 3–4 months |

**Prepared foods**

| | |
|---|---|
| Ready prepared meals, highly seasoned | 2–3 months |
| Ready prepared meals, average seasoning | 4–6 months |
| Cakes | 4–6 months |
| Bread, all kinds | 2–3 months |
| Other yeast products and pastries | 3–4 months |

*\* Chart published by kind permission of the Food Safety Advisory Centre*

## USING A MICROWAVE

Health advisers do not recommend using a microwave for reheating as the food heats up unevenly but if you decide to microwave baby food then make sure you stir the food thoroughly after cooking. Let the dish stand for 2–3 minutes before stirring again so that "hot spots" are well stirred into the mixture, and always check the temperature before serving. Choose the type of dish carefully as some pottery dishes can get very hot; plastic or pyrex dishes are the most successful in the microwave, heating food quickly but staying relatively cool themselves.

*Top: All parents will find the microwave incredibly helpful and time-saving. It can be used for heating milk and drinks (for toddlers – not newborns), for defrosting, reheating and cooking preprepared foods.*

1 Cover dish with plastic wrap, pierce and place in oven.

2 When cooked, remove and stir.

## MICROWAVING TIPS

• Never warm milk for a newborn or young baby in the microwave.
• For older children warm milk in a bottle without the nipple or an uncovered feeder beaker for 30–45 seconds. Stir well and always test the temperature of the milk (*not* the temperature of the container) before serving to make sure that the milk is an even and comfortable temperature. Do also seek advice from your pediatrician.
• To defrost ice cubes of baby food, press three into a baby dish, cover with plastic wrap and thaw in the microwave on Defrost (30%) setting for 1 to 2 minutes. Stir well then re-cover and microwave on High (100%) for 1 minute. Stir well to avoid hot spots then test the temperature.

# Root Vegetable Purée

**Makes: 2½ cups**

4oz carrot

4oz parsnip

4oz rutabaga

4oz potato

1¼ cups formula

1 Trim and peel the carrot, parsnip, rutabaga and potato and place in a colander. Rinse under cold water, drain and chop.

2 Place the chopped vegetables in a saucepan with the formula then bring to a boil, cover and simmer for 20 minutes or until they are very soft.

3 Purée or strain the vegetables until they are smooth.

4 Spoon a little into a bowl. Test the temperature and cool if necessary, before serving.

5 Cover the remaining food and refrigerate as soon as possible. Use within 24 hours.

● Suitable for freezing.

TIP
Thin the purée with a little extra formula if your baby prefers a very soft purée.

# Mixed Vegetable Purée

**Makes: 2½ cups**

| 4oz carrot |
| 6oz potato |
| 4oz broccoli |
| 2oz green cabbage |
| 1¼ cups formula |

**1** Peel the carrot and potato, rinse, chop and place in a saucepan. Wash the broccoli and cabbage and cut the broccoli into florets, the stems into slices and shred the cabbage finely.

**2** Add the formula to the carrot and potato, bring to a boil then cover and simmer for 10 minutes.

**3** Add the broccoli stems and florets and cabbage and cook, covered, for 10 minutes until all the vegetables are tender.

**4** Purée or strain the vegetables until smooth.

**5** Spoon a little into a bowl. Test the temperature and cool if necessary, before serving.

**6** Cover the remaining food and refrigerate as soon as possible. Use within 24 hours.

• Suitable for freezing.

# Carrot and Lentil Purée

**Makes: 2½ cups**

| |
| --- |
| 12oz carrots |
| 6oz potato |
| ¼ cup red lentils |
| ½ tsp ground coriander |
| 1¼ cups formula |

1 Trim and peel the carrots and potato and then chop into small cubes and place in a saucepan. Rinse the lentils thoroughly, discarding any black pieces.

2 Add the lentils, coriander and formula to the pan and bring to a boil, then cover and simmer for 40 minutes, until the lentils are very soft. Add a little extra boiling water if necessary.

**TIP**
The mixture thickens on cooling so any remaining mixture will need to be thinned slightly with a little formula before reheating for the next meal.

3 Purée or strain the vegetable and lentil mixture until smooth.

4 Spoon a little into a bowl. Test the temperature and cool if necessary, before serving.

5 Cover the remaining purée and refrigerate as soon as possible. Use within 24 hours.

● Suitable for freezing.

# Red Bell Pepper and Rice Purée

**Makes: 2½ cups**

¼ cup long grain rice

1¼ cups formula

3oz red bell pepper

3oz zucchini

2oz celery

**1** Place the rice and formula in a saucepan, bring to a boil and simmer, uncovered, for 5 minutes.

**2** Discard the core and seeds from the bell pepper and trim the zucchini and celery. Place the vegetables in a colander and rinse under cold water then chop them into small pieces.

**3** Add the vegetables to the rice mixture, bring to a boil, cover and simmer for about 10 minutes or until the rice is soft.

• Suitable for freezing.

**4** Purée or strain the rice and vegetable mixture until smooth.

**5** Spoon a little into a bowl. Test the temperature and cool if necessary, before serving.

**6** Cover the remaining food and refrigerate as soon as possible. Use within 24 hours.

# Parsnip and Broccoli Purée

**Makes: 2½ cups**

| |
|---|
| 8oz parsnips |
| 4oz broccoli |
| 1¼ cups formula |

**1** Trim and peel the parsnips and place in a colander with the broccoli. Rinse the parsnips and broccoli under cold water. Chop the parsnips and cut the broccoli into florets, slicing the stems.

**2** Put the parsnips in a saucepan with the formula, bring to a boil, then cover and simmer for about 10 minutes.

**3** Add the broccoli and simmer for 10 minutes more, until the vegetables are soft.

**4** Purée or strain the vegetable mixture to make a completely smooth purée.

**5** Spoon a little into a bowl. Test the temperature and cool if necessary, before serving.

**6** Cover the remaining food and refrigerate as soon as possible. Use within 24 hours.

• Suitable for freezing.

# Turkey, Carrot and Corn Purée

**Makes: 2½ cups**

6oz potato

6oz carrot

4oz boneless, skinless turkey breast

⅓ cup frozen corn

1¼ cups formula

**1** Trim and peel the potato and carrot, rinse under cold water and then chop into small cubes.

**2** Rinse the turkey and cut into thin strips. Place in a small saucepan with the potato and carrot.

**TIP**
Bring the turkey and vegetable mixture to a boil in a flameproof casserole and transfer to a preheated 350°F oven and cook for 1¼ hours if preferred.

**3** Add the corn and formula. Cover and simmer for 20 minutes, until the turkey is cooked. Purée or strain the mixture until completely smooth.

**4** Spoon a little into a bowl. Test the temperature and cool if necessary, before serving.

**5** Cover the remaining food and refrigerate. Use within 24 hours.

● Suitable for freezing.

# Chicken and Parsnip Purée

**Makes: 2½ cups**

12oz parsnips

4oz boneless, skinless chicken breast

1¼ cups formula

**1** Peel the parsnips, and trim the woody tops and bottoms. Rinse and chop roughly.

**2** Rinse the chicken under cold water and cut into small pieces.

**3** Place the parsnips, chicken and formula in a saucepan. Cover and simmer for 20 minutes or until the parsnips are tender.

**4** Purée or strain the chicken and parsnip mixture until smooth.

**5** Spoon into a bowl. Test the temperature and cool if necessary, before serving.

**6** Cover the remaining food and refrigerate as soon as possible. Use within 24 hours.

• Suitable for freezing.

TIP
For a very smooth purée, drain all the liquid into a blender and add half the solids, blend until smooth then add the remaining ingredients. If using a food processor, add all the solids and a little liquid, process until smooth then add the remaining liquid.

# Chicken and Leek Purée

**Makes: 2½ cups**

| |
|---|
| 2oz leek |
| 10oz potatoes |
| 4oz boneless, skinless chicken breast |
| 1¼ cups formula |

4 Bring the mixture to a boil, cover with a lid and simmer gently for 20 minutes, until the potatoes are just tender. Purée or strain the mixture until it is completely smooth.

5 Spoon a little into a bowl. Test the temperature and cool if necessary, before serving. Use within 24 hours.

● Suitable for freezing.

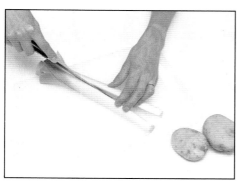

1 Halve the leek lengthwise and rinse under running water to remove any dirt or grit.

2 Peel the potatoes and cut into dice. Rinse the chicken and cut into pieces and thinly slice the leek.

3 Place the vegetables and chicken in a saucepan with the formula.

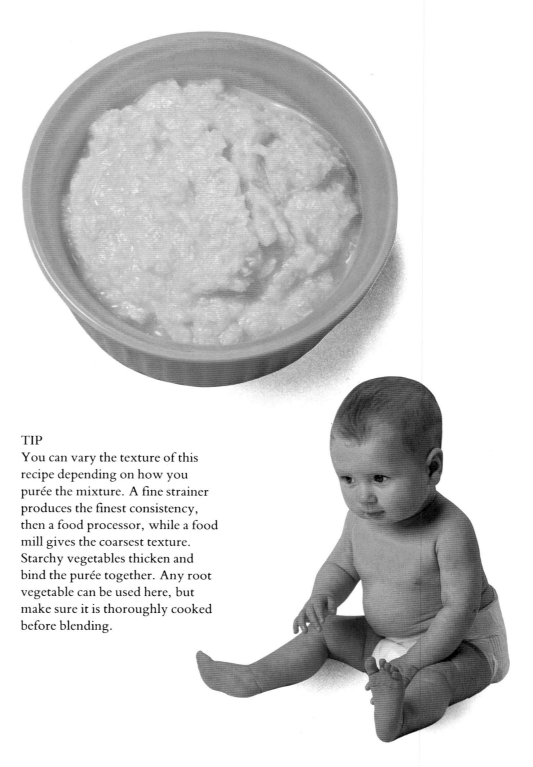

TIP
You can vary the texture of this recipe depending on how you purée the mixture. A fine strainer produces the finest consistency, then a food processor, while a food mill gives the coarsest texture. Starchy vegetables thicken and bind the purée together. Any root vegetable can be used here, but make sure it is thoroughly cooked before blending.

# Fish and Zucchini Purée

**Makes: 2½ cups**

| |
|---|
| 10oz potatoes |
| 6oz zucchini |
| 4oz trout fillet |
| 1 cup formula |

1 Peel the potatoes, trim the zucchini and rinse under cold water. Dice the potatoes and cut the zucchini into slices.

2 Place the vegetables in a saucepan. Rinse the trout and arrange on top, then pour over the formula. Bring to a boil, cover and simmer for 15 minutes, until the potatoes and fish are cooked.

3 Lift the trout out of the pan and peel off the skin. Break it into pieces with a knife and fork, checking carefully for any bones.

4 Purée or strain the fish, the vegetables and the liquid until quite smooth.

5 Spoon a little into a bowl. Test the temperature and cool if necessary, before serving.

6 Cover any remaining food and refrigerate as soon as possible. Use within 24 hours.

• Suitable for freezing.

# Cod and Corn Purée

**Makes: 2½ cups**

| |
|---|
| 12oz potatoes |
| 3½oz frozen cod |
| ¼ cup frozen peas |
| 2 tbsp frozen corn |
| 1¼ cups formula |

1 Peel and rinse the potatoes and cut into even–sized pieces. Place in a saucepan with the fish, peas, corn and formula.

2 Bring to a boil, cover and simmer for 15 minutes until the potatoes are very tender.

3 Lift the fish out of the pan and break into pieces with a knife and fork, checking carefully and removing any small bones.

4 Purée or strain the fish, vegetables and cooking liquid until completely smooth.

5 Spoon a little into a bowl. Test the temperature and cool if necessary, before serving.

6 Cover the remaining purée and refrigerate as soon as possible. Use within 24 hours.

• Suitable for freezing.

# Apple Ambrosia

**Makes: 1¼ cups**

| 1 eating apple |
| 1oz rice cereal |
| 1¼ cups formula |

**1** Quarter, core and peel the apple. Slice and place in a saucepan with the cereal and formula.

**2** Bring to a boil then simmer gently for 10–12 minutes until the cereal is soft, stirring occasionally with a wooden spoon.

**4** Spoon a little into a bowl. Test the temperature and cool if necessary, before serving. Cover the remaining purée and refrigerate as soon as possible. Use within 24 hours.

**VARIATION**
**Chocolate Pudding**
Cook the cereal as above but without the apple. Stir 1oz milk chocolate chips and 1tbsp superfine sugar into the hot cereal and then purée until smooth. Spoon into small dishes and cool as necessary.

**3** Purée the apple and cereal mixture until completely smooth.

# Fruit Salad Purée

**Makes: 1½ cups**

| |
|---|
| 1 nectarine or peach |
| 1 eating apple |
| 1 ripe pear |
| 1oz fresh or frozen raspberries or strawberries |

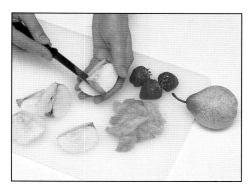

**1** Halve the nectarine or peach, discard the pit then peel and chop. Quarter, core and peel the apple and pear and slice thinly.

**2** Put the prepared fruits, the raspberries or strawberries and 1 tbsp water in a saucepan. Cover and simmer for 10 minutes until the fruit is soft.

**3** Strain the mixture, or process and then press through a strainer to remove the berry seeds. Discard the seeds.

**4** Spoon a little into a baby bowl. Test the temperature and cool if necessary, before serving.

**5** Cover the remaining purée and refrigerate as soon as possible. Use within 24 hours.

- Suitable for freezing.

TIP
Babies tend to eat smaller quantities of dessert so it is best to freeze purée in a sterilized ice cube tray. Transfer the cubes to a plastic bag once frozen.

### VARIATION
### Peach Melon Purée
To make ¾ cup, take 1 ripe peach and ¼ ripe canteloupe melon. Peel and halve the peach, discard the pit and cut up the fruit. Scoop the seeds out of the melon and cut away the skin. Roughly chop the melon into pieces.

Purée or strain the fruit until completely smooth. Spoon a little into a bowl and serve.

# STAGE 3: SIX TO NINE MONTHS

Baby purée can be processed or mashed but still needs to be fairly soft. A few small bits can be introduced, but be guided by your baby and adjust the textures as required. As always, don't rush things and go at your baby's pace.

If you like, let your baby hold a second spoon while you are feeding her to help develop coordination. This is the first step toward self-feeding.

All the recipes from the previous section can still be made for your growing baby; just adjust the texture so that foods are slightly coarser.

## *Suitable Foods*

**FOODS TO INCLUDE**
- wheat-based foods, pasta, bread – first fingers of toast or bread sticks
- breakfast cereals such as oatmeal or Wheatina made up with cows' milk
- cows' milk and dairy foods, e.g. yogurt, cottage cheese, mild Cheddar and Edam cheese
- red meat, but make sure you trim off fat and gristle
- hard-boiled egg yolk
- citrus fruits
- fingers of cooked carrot, broccoli
- smooth peanut butter

Breakfast cereals

Mild cheeses

Yogurt

Lean red meat

Cottage cheese

Bread

Fish

Pasta

Citrus fruits

Cooked egg yolk

Peanut butter

Broccoli and carrot

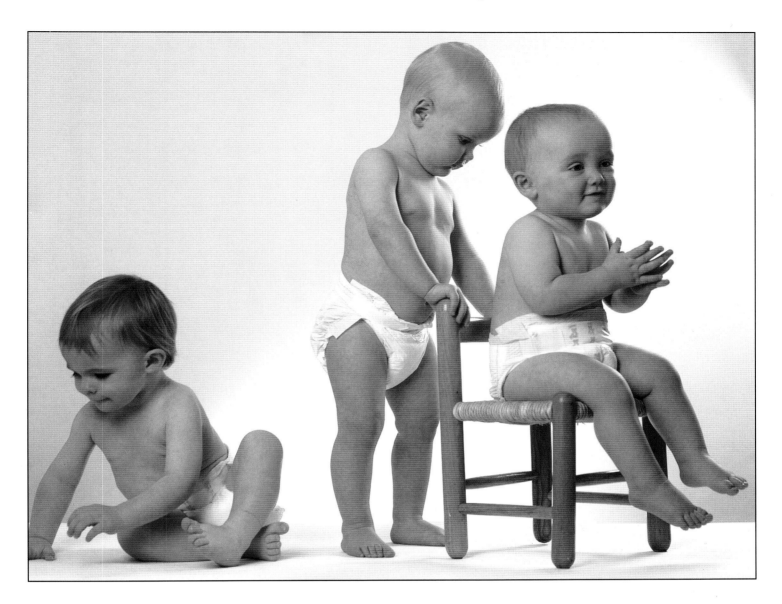

Above: *At six to nine months your baby will be delighted to try pasta and cheese.*

## FOODS TO AVOID
- egg white
- whole or chopped nuts
- canned fish in brine
- organ meats – liver, kidney
- chilies and other very spicy foods
- salty foods
- sugary foods

Right: *There is still a wide range of fatty, salty and spicy foods that must be avoided.*

# Choosing a Highchair

There is a surprisingly wide choice of highchairs available in a range of finishes, colors and price levels so make sure you shop around before you buy.

## CONVERTIBLE CHAIRS

Designed for babies between four weeks and six months, these chairs can convert from a highchair into a swing and some models into a baby chair and rocker too. It is best to buy one of these when the baby is very young so that you get maximum use from it. The only disadvantage may be the space required for the frame. The ease in converting from one type of chair to another varies from model to model, so you would be well advised to practice in the shop before buying. Most chairs have white painted frames.

## THREE-IN-ONE CHAIRS

Various designs on the market convert into a separate chair, chair and table or highchair. Some simply clip apart while others require a little help with a screwdriver. There are good rigid structures available with a wide range of decorative seat patterns. They are available in wood or white finishes. The low chair is suitable for children up to four years old if used without the tray.

## ELEVATOR CHAIRS

These slightly more expensive chairs convert from a highchair to a low chair. Some models have adjustable tray settings to fit a growing child. The frames are mostly available in white metal, with attractive seating.

**Three-in-one type**

**Elevator type**

TIPS
● For maximum use of a highchair, buy a booster cushion for the early days when your baby first begins to use the chair. Adjust the tray position as well, if possible.
● Check that the highchair is easy to clean – dried-on cereal can be impossible to clean off. Look out for possible dirt traps on the seat or around the tray fixing.
● Make sure that the chair is sturdy and rigid – it will need to withstand considerable wear.

Above: *A portable clip-on chair.*

● If using a clip-on highchair make sure that the table is suitable and will be able to withstand the weight of your child. Never, in any circumstances, fix onto glass.

## FOLDING CHAIRS

These less expensive chairs, available in wood or white finishes, usually fold up in a scissor movement. Some can be folded crosswise for packing into the trunk of the car. Before buying, check how easy they are to fold out and up and make sure the frame is rigid when opened out.

**Folding type**

## COUNTRY-TYPE CHAIRS

These are sturdy wooden highchairs usually with a wooden tray and attractive cottage-style spindle features. The seat can be hard for baby so it is best to buy a fitted chair cushion.

## PORTABLE CHAIRS

There are two main types available:
● a very simple cloth tie, useful for visiting friends or eating out as it will fold up and fit in a bag. However, it is not really suitable for everyday use as the child is literally tied on to the chair and so cannot reach the table to feed himself.
● clip-on seats where the frames are placed under and over the edge of a dining table. Check that the table is strong enough and is not likely to overbalance before you put your baby in the chair.

1 Undo the tray catches by pressing both sides at once, and fold the tray upward.

2 Undo the side catches that keep the frame rigid so the chair can scissor in two.

3 This allows you to fold the chair over onto itself: the design is incredibly neat and compact.

4 It is now ready for storing, putting out of the way, or popping into the trunk of the car.

TIPS
● Always use a safety harness. Although most highchairs have a three-point lap strap you will probably have to buy straps that will go around your baby's body and clip onto the chair. It is amazing how quickly a baby learns to wriggle out of a highchair when you're not looking.
● Never leave a child in a highchair unattended.

Above: *Always strap your baby in tightly.*

# Shepherd's Pie Mash

**Makes: 2½ cups**

| 2 tomatoes |
| --- |
| ¼ onion |
| 8oz potato |
| 2oz button mushrooms |
| 4oz lean ground beef |
| 1 cup water |
| 1 tbsp ketchup |
| pinch of dried mixed herbs |

1 Make a cross cut in each tomato, put in a small bowl and cover with boiling water. Let stand for 1 minute and then drain and peel off the skins. Cut into quarters and scoop out the seeds.

2 Finely chop the onion, chop the potato and slice the mushrooms.

3 Fry the beef in a dry skillet. Brown for 5 minutes, stirring continuously.

● Suitable for freezing.

4 Add the tomatoes, potato, mushrooms and onion and cook for 3 minutes more. Stir well to blend all the flavors together.

5 Add the water, ketchup and herbs. Bring to a boil then reduce the heat, cover and simmer for 40 minutes until the meat and vegetables are tender.

6 Process or mash the meat and vegetables just enough to give the desired consistency.

7 Spoon a little into a bowl. Test the temperature and cool if necessary, before serving.

8 Cover and refrigerate as soon as possible. Use within 24 hours.

# Braised Beef and Carrot Mash

**Makes: 2½ cups**

| |
|---|
| 6oz potato |
| 8oz carrots |
| ¼ onion |
| 6oz stewing beef |
| 1¼ cups water |
| pinch of dried mixed herbs |

**1** Preheat the oven to 350°F. Peel and chop the potato, carrots and onion and place in a flameproof casserole.

**2** Rinse the beef, cut away any fat and gristle and cut into small cubes using a sharp knife.

**3** Add the meat, water and herbs to the casserole, bring to a boil and then cover and cook in the oven for 1½ hours or until the meat is tender and the vegetables are soft.

**4** Process or mash the ingredients to the desired consistency and spoon a little into a bowl. Test the temperature and cool if necessary, before serving.

**5** Cover any unused food and refrigerate as soon as possible. Use within 24 hours.

● Suitable for freezing.

TIP
Replace the carrots with any other root vegetable such as parsnip or rutabaga, if wished.

# Lamb and Vegetable Mash

**Makes: 2½ cups**

| |
|---|
| 4oz potato |
| 4oz carrot |
| 4oz rutabaga |
| 2oz leek |
| 4oz boneless lamb |
| 1¼ cup water |
| pinch of dried rosemary |

**1** Peel the potato, carrot and rutabaga, rinse and chop into small cubes. Halve the leek lengthwise, rinse and slice. Place all the vegetables in a saucepan.

**2** Rinse the lamb under cold water and chop into small pieces, discarding any fat.

**3** Add the meat to the pan with the water and rosemary. Bring to a boil, cover and simmer for 30 minutes or until the lamb is thoroughly cooked.

**4** Process or mash the ingredients to the desired consistency.

**5** Spoon a little into a bowl, test the temperature and cool if necessary, before serving.

**6** Cover the remaining food and refrigerate as soon as possible. Use within 24 hours.

• Suitable for freezing.

# Lamb and Lentil Mash

**Makes: 2½ cups**

| |
|---|
| 4oz boneless lamb |
| 4oz rutabaga |
| 1 celery stalk |
| 2 tbsp red lentils |
| 1 tbsp ketchup |
| 1½ cups water |

**1** Rinse the lamb under cold water, trim off any fat and chop into small pieces. Peel the rutabaga, place in a colander with the celery and rinse with cold water. Chop into cubes and place in a saucepan.

**2** Put the lentils in a strainer and rinse under cold water, picking out any black pieces. Add to the pan with the lamb and ketchup.

**3** Add the water, bring to a boil, then cover and simmer for 40 minutes or until the lentils are soft. Add extra water during cooking if necessary, then process or mash to give the desired consistency.

**4** Spoon a little into a bowl, test the temperature and cool if necessary, before serving.

**5** Cover the remaining food and refrigerate as soon as possible. Use within 24 hours.

● Suitable for freezing.

**VARIATION**
Substitute green lentils or split peas for the red lentils and a small zucchini for the celery stalk.

# Pork and Green Bean Mash

**Makes: 1⅞ cups**

4oz boneless, lean pork

4oz potato

4oz carrot

3oz green beans

pinch of dried sage

1½ cups water

1 Rinse the pork under cold water, trim away any fat and gristle and chop into small cubes.

2 Peel the potato and carrot, trim the beans, rinse and chop.

TIP
Sugar peas or broccoli make tasty substitutes for green beans. Look for ready prepared diced pork in the supermarket. Cut the meat into smaller pieces and make sure to remove any gristle before cooking.

3 Put the pork, potato and carrot in a saucepan with the sage and water. Bring to a boil, cover and simmer for 30 minutes.

4 Add the beans and cook, covered, for 10 minutes more until all the vegetables are tender.

5 Process or mash to the desired consistency, then spoon a little into a bowl. Test the temperature before serving.

6 Cover and refrigerate as soon as possible. Use within 24 hours.

● Suitable for freezing.

**VARIATION**
Instead of the pork, use any lean meat in this recipe, such as chicken or turkey. Add broad beans, with the outer skins removed, in place of the green beans.

# Pork and Apple Mash

**Makes: 2½ cups**

| |
|---|
| 6oz boneless, lean pork |
| 6oz potato |
| 6oz rutabaga or parsnip |
| ¼ onion |
| ½ eating apple |
| 1¼ cups water |
| pinch of dried sage |

**1** Preheat the oven to 350°F. Rinse the pork under cold water, trim away any fat and gristle then chop into small pieces. Peel and chop the vegetables. Peel, core and chop the apple.

**2** Put the meat, vegetables, apple, water and sage in a flameproof casserole, cover and bring to a boil stirring once or twice.

**3** Cover and cook in the oven for 1¼ hours until the meat is tender, then process or mash to the desired consistency.

**4** Spoon a little into a bowl, test the temperature and cool if necessary, before serving.

**5** Cover the remaining food and refrigerate as soon as possible. Use within 24 hours.

● Suitable for freezing.

**TIP**
The mixture can be cooked in a saucepan on the stove for 40 minutes if preferred.

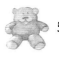 

# Fish and Rice Mash

**Makes: 2½ cups**

| |
|---|
| ¼ cup long grain rice |
| 2 tbsp frozen peas |
| 1½ cups formula |
| 3oz frozen cod |
| 2 hard-boiled egg yolks |

**1** Place the rice, peas, formula and fish in a saucepan, bring to a boil, cover and simmer for 15 minutes, until the fish is cooked and the rice is soft.

**2** Lift the fish out of the pan and break into pieces with a knife and fork, checking for bones.

**3** Stir the fish into the rice mixture and add the egg yolks.

**TIP**
Peas can be quite difficult to mash. Check the mixture before serving as whole peas are difficult for a baby to chew.

**4** Mash with a fork to the desired consistency. Alternatively blend in a food processor, blender or press through a strainer.

**5** Spoon a little into a bowl, test the temperature and cool if necessary, before serving.

**6** Cover the remaining food and refrigerate as soon as possible. Use within 24 hours.

● Suitable for freezing.

# Mediterranean Vegetable Mash

**Makes: 2½ cups**

| |
|---|
| 3 tomatoes |
| 6oz zucchini |
| 3oz button mushrooms |
| 4oz red bell pepper |
| 4 tsp ketchup |
| 1 cup water |
| pinch of dried mixed herbs |
| 1½oz small pasta |

**3** Rinse and slice the zucchini and mushrooms. Chop the pepper.

**4** Put the vegetables in a saucepan with the ketchup, water and herbs. Cover and simmer for 10 minutes or until tender.

**5** Meanwhile cook the pasta in boiling water for 8–10 minutes until tender. Drain.

**6** Mix the vegetables and pasta together and process or mash.

**7** Spoon a little into a bowl, test the temperature and cool if necessary, before serving.

**8** Cover the remaining food and refrigerate. Use within 24 hours.

• Suitable for freezing.

**1** Make a cross cut in each tomato, put in a small bowl and cover with boiling water. Leave for 1 minute then drain and peel off the skins. Cut into quarters and scoop out the seeds from the tomatoes.

**2** Trim the zucchini and mushrooms and cut away the core and seeds from the bell pepper.

TIP
For adventurous eaters add ½ clove crushed garlic at Step 3.

# Pasta and Vegetable Mash

**Makes: 2½ cups**

| |
|---|
| 4oz carrot |
| 2oz Brussels sprouts |
| 1oz green beans |
| 2 tbsp frozen corn |
| 2oz small pasta |
| 1½ cups formula |
| 2oz mild Cheddar cheese |

1 Peel the carrot, discard any discolored outer leaves from the sprouts and trim the beans. Rinse and then chop into pieces.

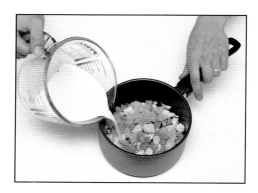

2 Place the vegetables, corn, pasta and formula in a saucepan, bring to a boil and then simmer, uncovered, for 12–15 minutes until the pasta is cooked.

**TIP**
Vary the vegetables depending on what you have available.

3 Grate the cheese and add to the vegetables, stirring until the cheese has completely melted.

4 Process or mash just enough to give the desired consistency, then spoon a little into a bowl. Test the temperature and cool if necessary, before serving.

5 Cover the remaining food and refrigerate as soon as possible. Use within 24 hours.

● Suitable for freezing.

# Apple and Orange Custard

**Makes: 1 cup**

2 eating apples

1 tsp grated orange zest and
  1 tbsp orange juice

1 tbsp instant vanilla custard

1 tsp superfine sugar

2/3 cup formula

**1** Quarter, core and peel the apples. Slice and place the apples in a saucepan with the orange zest and juice.

**2** Cover and cook gently for 10 minutes, stirring occasionally until the apples are soft.

**3** Blend the instant custard and sugar with a little of the formula to make a smooth paste. Bring the remaining formula to a boil and stir into the custard mixture.

**4** Return the custard to the pan and slowly bring to a boil, stirring until thickened and smooth.

**5** Process or mash the apple to the desired consistency. Add the custard and stir to mix.

**6** Spoon a little into a bowl, test the temperature and cool if necessary, before serving.

**7** Cover the remaining food and refrigerate as soon as possible. Use within 24 hours.

• Suitable for freezing.

# Orchard Fruit Dessert

**Makes: 1⅞ cups**

| |
| --- |
| 1 ripe pear |
| 8oz ripe plums |
| 1 tbsp superfine sugar |
| 1 tbsp instant vanilla custard |
| ⅔ cup formula |

**1** Quarter, core, peel and slice the pear. Wash the plums, then cut in half, pit and slice.

**2** Put the fruit in a saucepan with 1 tbsp water and 2 tsp of the sugar. Cover and cook gently for 10 minutes until soft.

**3** Blend the instant custard, remaining sugar and a little of the formula to a smooth paste.

**4** Bring the remaining formula to a boil and gradually stir into the custard mixture. Pour the custard back into the pan and bring to a boil, stirring, until it is both thickened and smooth.

**5** Process or mash the fruit to the desired consistency and stir in the custard. Spoon a little into a bowl, test the temperature and cool if necessary, before serving.

**6** Cover the remaining custard and refrigerate as soon as possible. Use within 24 hours.

● Suitable for freezing.

# Peach Melba Yogurt

**Makes: ¾ cup**

1 ripe peach

1oz fresh or frozen raspberries

1 tbsp confectioner's sugar

4oz plain yogurt

1 Halve the peach, discard the pit then peel and slice. Place in a saucepan with the raspberries and 1 tbsp water.

2 Cover and cook gently for 10 minutes until soft.

3 Purée and press through a strainer to remove the pips.

TIP
The finished dessert is not suitable for freezing although the sweetened fruit purée can be frozen successfully in sections of an ice cube tray. Defrost cubes of purée and mix each cube with about 1 tbsp yogurt.

4 Set aside to cool then stir in the sugar and swirl in the yogurt. Spoon a little into a baby dish.

5 Cover the remaining food and refrigerate as soon as possible. Use within 24 hours.

**VARIATION**
**Bananarama**
To make a single portion, use ½ a small banana and 1 tbsp of plain yogurt. Mash the banana until smooth and add the yogurt. Stir to mix and serve immediately. Do not make this dessert in advance, as the banana will discolor while standing.

# STAGE 4: NINE TO TWELVE MONTHS

GRADUALLY PROGRESS FROM GROUND TO CHOPPED OR ROUGHLY MASHED FOOD. BY NOW YOUR BABY WILL BE ABLE TO JOIN IN WITH FAMILY MEALS AND EAT A LITTLE OF WHAT YOU ARE EATING. ENSURE THAT YOUR BABY IS EATING THREE MAIN MEALS AND TWO TO THREE SNACK MEALS PER DAY. YOUNG CHILDREN DEVELOP AT AN INCREDIBLY FAST RATE AND SO NEED TO EAT LITTLE AND OFTEN TO SUSTAIN ENERGY AND GROWTH LEVELS.

AGAIN FOODS FROM THE PREVIOUS SECTIONS CAN STILL BE SERVED TO YOUR BABY; JUST ADJUST THE TEXTURES AS NECESSARY.

## Suitable Foods

**FOODS TO INCLUDE**
- whole eggs
- finely ground nuts
- more flavorings – bouillon cubes if part of a family-size casserole

- greater selection of finger foods – slices of peeled fruit (such as apple or pear), cooked carrot sticks and cucumber sticks, small cubes of cooked chicken

- selection of foods from the four main food groups

**Apple, carrot and cucumber**

Left: *Finger foods – such as chopped vegetables and fruit pieces – come into their own at this age, and children love to help themselves.*

**Whole egg**

Above: *Inquisitive children love the time when they can join the family at the table.*

## FOODS TO AVOID
- keep salt to a minimum and omit if possible
- sugar: add just enough to make the food appetizing without being overly sweet
- honey
- fat: trim visible fat off raw meat, grill rather than fry
- organ meats – liver, kidney

Below: *Though now a very small list, there are still some foods it is important to omit.*

**Bouillon cubes**

**Ground nuts**

# I can feed myself!

Encouraging your baby to feed herself can be a truly messy business. Some babies are interested from a very early age and those little fingers seem to move like lightning grabbing the bowl or the spoon you're using to feed them with. While foods are still finely puréed, give your baby a second spoon to play with, leaving you more able to spoon in the real lunch.

As your baby grows offer her a few finger foods to hold and hopefully eat, while you continue to feed from a spoon. Cooked carrot sticks, broccoli and cauliflower florets are soft on a young mouth and easy to chew. As your baby grows you can introduce bread sticks and toast fingers.

Encourage your baby to pick up foods and as her coordination improves and she gets the idea, more food will actually go where it is intended. Try to cut down on the mess by rolling up your baby's sleeves and covering clothes with a large bib, preferably with sleeves.

Above: *A bib with sleeves.*

Remove any hair bands and have a wet washcloth at the ready.

Although it is tempting not to allow a baby to feed herself, try not to be frustrated by the mess. Babies who are encouraged to feed themselves will probably be more adventurous later on and you will probably find there is less mess than

## TEACHING YOUR BABY TO FEED ITSELF

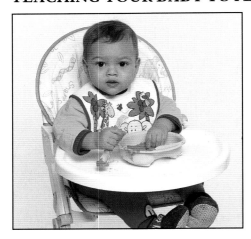

**1** Cover your baby well – this can be very messy! Give her a spoon of her own to play with.

**2** While you are feeding your baby, allow her to play with the food – with her hands or the spoon.

**3** Let your baby use the cup and spoon by herself. Don't worry about spillage – there are bound to be lots of slips at this stage.

**4** Keep tissues or a damp washcloth available and clean as you go. Be patient and take things slowly.

with a baby who is always spoon fed and keeps grabbing at the bowl. In addition, she will be able to join in your family meals and also give you the chance to eat your own meal before it goes cold.

## WHAT TO DO IF YOUR CHILD CHOKES
- Don't waste time trying to remove food from your baby's mouth unless it can be done easily.
- Turn your baby, head down, supporting her head with your forearm and slap firmly between the shoulder blades.
- If this does not work, try again.
- Don't hesitate to call your doctor or emergency services if worried.

Left: *It is a real delight when your baby can begin to feed independently. Not only can you start to eat with your baby, and relax a little more, but she will also enjoy setting her own pace and eating her meal in the order she chooses. At this stage the family can usually return to eating together around the table as a group.*

Above: *Don't be afraid to take quick, firm action in an emergency.*

## COPING WITH THE MESS
As babies grow so too does the amount of mess! It can seem incredible how just a few tablespoons of lunch can be spread across so many surfaces and so many items of clothing.
- Choose a large bib. Fabric bibs with a plastic liner are the most comfortable for babies to wear when tiny, moving on to a plastic pelican-style bib to catch the spills as they grow older. Check the back of your

Above: *A hard plastic "pelican" bib.*

baby's neck as these can rub.
- If you plan to feed your baby in the dining room, then protect the carpet with an old sheet, pieces of newspaper or plastic tablecloth or drop cloth. It is vital to take this with you if visiting friends.
- Give your baby a second spoon or small toy to play with so that she doesn't make a grab for the spoon you are using.

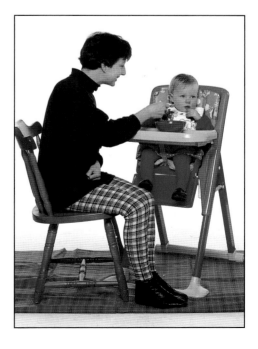

Above: *A plastic tablecloth or drop cloth on the floor will avoid carpet stains.*

## FINGER FOODS

Finger foods are not only fun to eat but help your baby's coordination. Snacks play an important part in a young child's diet as appetites may be small, but energy and growth needs are great. Choose foods that are nutrient dense and avoid sweet sugary snacks such as chocolate cookies.

Grapes

Plums

Celery      Carrots

Mini-sandwiches

Toast triangles

Chicken pieces      Fish fingers

Cheese cubes

Toast fingers      Ham

Above: *Your baby can eat at her own pace until she is full.*

### TIPS

• Always make sure baby is comfortable either on your lap or strapped into a baby chair or highchair.

• Check the temperature of the food and make sure it is not too hot.

• Change the texture of the food: some babies like quite wet mixtures, some hate lumps, some like a few lumps for interest, others prefer food they can pick up – tiny ham sandwiches, thick slices of grilled fish finger, even picking up peas and corn.

• Encourage your baby to feed herself; don't worry about mess – your baby is still learning – but just mop up sticky hands and face at the end.

• Try to keep calm. If your baby keeps spitting food out, you may find it less upsetting to offer store-bought food rather than homemade so you don't feel you've been wasting your time cooking.

• Try not to let your baby see you're upset or angry. Even a one-year-old can sense the power she can have over you.

• If solid meals are well established, give her a drink at the end of the meal so that she is not filled up with milk before she begins.

• Avoid cookies and sweets as your baby will soon learn that if she makes a fuss when the main dish is offered, then dessert will soon follow.

• Remember no baby will starve herself. Continue offering a variety of food and don't despair.

Above: *Give drinks at the end of the meal, or they will fill her up before she eats.*

# Coping with a fussy eater

All children are fussy eaters at some stage. If mealtimes are always calm and plates always clean then your family must be one in a million. Even very young children learn the power they have over their parents and mealtimes give them a great opportunity to exercise it. Here are some common problems and advice on how to deal with them.

## BABY SPITS OUT FOOD
You may be trying to wean your baby too soon or possibly she simply doesn't like the taste of the food. If you started with baby rice then go on to potato or parsnip purée or a little applesauce mixed into the baby rice. If that fails, your baby may simply not be ready for solids just yet. Try again in a week or two's time.

## BABY APPEARS TO GAG
Some babies just cannot cope with solids at first and may seem distressed and almost gag on the food. Try thinning down the food with a little more breast milk, formula or water, since the food may be too thick. Alternatively, you may be putting too much food on the spoon; try offering the baby a little less. If neither of these seems to help, stop solids and breast or bottle feed as usual, giving her plenty of reassuring cuddles. Try again in a few days' or weeks' time. If your baby is nearly six months old then don't hesitate to ask your doctor for advice.

## BABY SEEMS TO HAVE A SMALL APPETITE
Babies' appetites, like adults', vary enormously. Don't force feed your baby; if she's been eating well and then turns her head away or starts spitting it out, it's a pretty clear

Above: *Don't worry when you encounter resistance in feeding: there never has been a baby that likes all foods, all the time.*

Left: *If you have serious anxieties, see your doctor and get your baby's weight checked regularly.*

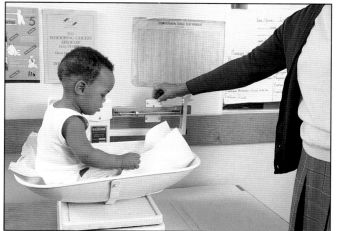

indication that she's had enough, even if the amount does seem very small to you. Resist the temptation to encourage the baby to clean the plate: it is never helpful to force

children of any age, and can be extremely counterproductive. If you're worried, talk to your pediatrician and regularly check your baby's weight.

# Going Vegetarian

A vegetarian diet can provide all the necessary nutrients for health and vitality, but it is important to balance the baby's diet to ensure that she receives adequate supplies of protein, vitamins D and B12, calcium and iron.

The basic guidelines are the same as for weaning any other baby; introduce flavors slowly and be guided by your baby. The biggest differences are obviously in the type of foods offered. Instead of obtaining protein from meat and fish, your baby will receive it from other protein-rich food. These include eggs, legumes, split lentils and grains, finely ground nuts or nut creams, sunflower seed spread, milk and dairy products and vegetarian cheese where available.

Vegetarians need to make sure that sufficient iron is included in their baby's diet. If she is over six months, offer prune juice, puréed apricots, molasses, refined lentils and cereals, particularly fortified breakfast cereals. Green vegetables and well-mashed beans, if over eight months, are also a good source of iron. Vitamin C aids absorption of iron from plant sources so make sure you serve fresh green vegetables or fruit in the meal. Your doctor may also feel it beneficial for your baby to take vitamin drops.

If you plan to bring the baby up as a vegan and so omit dairy products and eggs from the diet, then it is vital

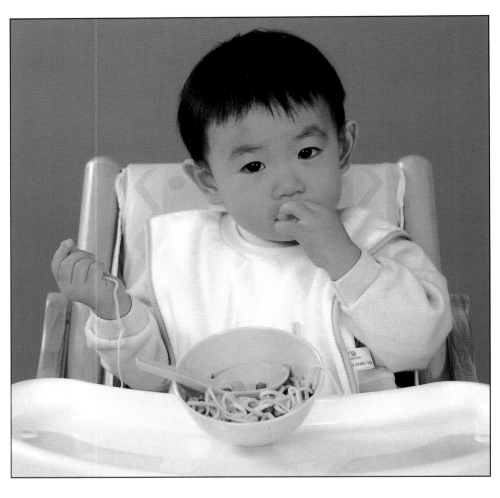

to consult your doctor or dietician.

Vegetarian diets tend to be bulky and lower in calories than a diet containing meats so make sure you include foods that are protein and calorie rich, with little or no fiber, such as eggs, milk and cheese. These can be mixed with smaller quantities of vegetables, fruit and cereals. Fiber-rich foods can also be difficult

Above: *Raising your child as a vegetarian takes special planning and care.*

for a child to digest as many nutrients may pass straight through.

To ensure your baby is getting the correct amount of vitamins, minerals and food energy her diet should include foods from the four groups on the opposite page:

**Oranges**

**Carrots**

**Cucumber**

**Grapes**

**Cereals and grains:** rice around four months; pasta, bread, oats, and breakfast cereals from six months.

**Fruit and vegetables:** begin with potato, carrot, apple and pear around four months, progressing to stronger-flavored foods as your baby develops.

**Dairy produce:** including milk, cheese and yogurt from six months. *Note:* Make sure cheese is rennet-free. If you are unsure, ask the delicatessen assistant, or check the package if pre-packed.

**Beans and legumes:** split peas and cooked lentils from five or six months. Gradual introduction of tofu, smooth peanut butter, hard-boiled egg yolks from six months. Well cooked mashed dried beans and peas and finely ground nuts from nine months. Do not give whole nuts to the under fives.

To make sure your baby is thriving and happy, irrespective of the type of diet, make sure you check your baby's weight at regular intervals at the pediatrician's.

**Baby lentils**

**Split peas**

**Lentils**

# The Importance of a Varied Diet

Once your baby progresses to more varied fruit and vegetable purées, you are really beginning to lay down the foundations for a healthy eating pattern and sound nutritional habits that will take your baby through childhood and into adult life.

It is vitally important to include portions of food from each of the four main food groups per day. But do make sure that the types of food you choose are suitable for the age of your child.

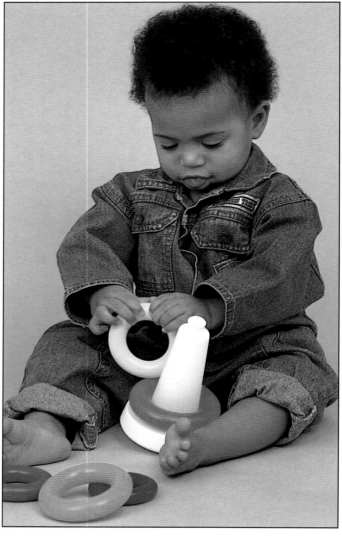

*Left: Your baby is now at the age where the diet can and should be as diverse as any adult's. Variety is crucial for health reasons, and also has the benefit of allowing you many options for tempting and maintaining the kind of interest in all types of food that will ensure that good eating habits develop for the future.*

**Group 1:** *Cereals, bread, potatoes, rice and pasta*

**Group 2:** *Fruit and vegetables* – bland tastes to start, such as potato, rutabaga and parsnip, then stronger flavors

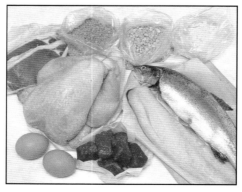

**Group 3:** *Meat and meat alternatives* – meat, poultry, fish, eggs, legumes (peas, beans and lentils), tofu, finely ground nuts

**Group 4:** *Milk and milk products* – milk, including soya milk, cheese, yogurt (plain at first, then flavored)

There are two more food groups that add palatability to the diet as well as contributing energy.

**Group 5:** *Sugars*

**Group 6:** *Fats and oils*

It is not recommended you add sugar to baby foods or give lots of sugary drinks, particularly in the early days of weaning. Many of us have an inherent need for sweetness but to cater to this without building in bad habits try and include foods in the diet that are naturally sweet. Choose eating apples instead of very tart cooking apples, mix bananas or ripe apricots with sharper-tasting fruits.

For those foods that are very tart try and add 1 tsp sugar per portion, so they become palatable without being overly sweet. Given the choice your baby would prefer sweet flavors to savory so make sure you include a good range of tastes in the diet. Too much sugar or sweetened

foods or drinks at this stage could lead to tooth decay before the teeth are even through.

Try to avoid offering cookies as a mid-morning or afternoon snack. Try to encourage your baby to eat:
- a piece of banana
- a plain bread roll
- a few triangles of toast
- a milky drink
- a small container of yogurt

Watch the amounts of fat and oil you include in the diet. Avoid frying especially when preparing first foods as young babies have difficulty digesting such foods. As your baby develops, you can spread toast fingers with a little butter or margarine or offer a few oven-baked "fries" as easy-to-hold finger foods. Maintain the milk feedings and introduce whole cows' milk after one year as the main drink of the day. Don't be tempted to serve skim milk as the valuable fat-soluble vitamins A and D will be lost, and your baby may not get the energy needed for growth.

### HOMEMADE OR MANUFACTURED FOODS?
Most mothers use a combination of the two. Store-bought baby foods are convenient and often easier to use if going out for the day or until your baby's meals coincide with the rest

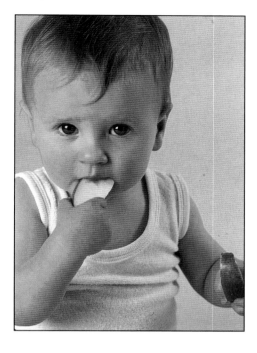

Above: *A piece of fruit or chopped vegetable is always preferable to a cookie.*

of the family. Jarred baby foods can be useful in the very early days when baby is eating only a teaspoon of food at each meal. On the other hand, homemade foods can be batch cooked or made with some of the ingredients from the main family meal and are often less trouble than you would expect. Added to this is the satisfaction of knowing your baby has eaten a wholesome meal and hopefully is acquiring a taste for home cooking.

Left: *Don't always assume that all homemade foods are better and more nutritious than all manufactured foods. There are now some excellent products available for purchase that can save you time and effort and add hugely to your repertoire without any loss of dietary values.*

# Lamb and Couscous

**Makes: 3⅓ cups**

| |
| --- |
| 4oz carrot |
| 4oz rutabaga |
| ¼ onion |
| 6oz boneless lamb |
| 1 tsp oil |
| 2 tsp tomato or vegetable paste |
| 2 tbsp currants or raisins |
| 1¼ cups water |
| 2oz couscous |

**1** Peel the carrot, rutabaga and onion, rinse and chop. Rinse the lamb, trim off any fat, and chop.

**2** Heat the oil in a saucepan, and sauté the lamb until browned.

**3** Add the vegetables, cook for 2 minutes then stir in the paste, currants and water. Cover and simmer for 25 minutes.

**4** Rinse the couscous in a strainer. Cover and steam the couscous over the lamb pan for 5 minutes.

**5** Chop or process the lamb mixture to the desired consistency. Fluff up the couscous with a fork and add to the lamb mixture stirring well.

**6** Spoon a little into a bowl, test the temperature and cool if necessary, before serving.

**7** Cover the remaining food and refrigerate as soon as possible. Use within 24 hours.

● Suitable for freezing.

TIP
Vegetable paste can be found in some specialty stores. Otherwise substitute tomato paste.

# Paprika Pork

**Makes: 2½ cups**

| |
|---|
| 6oz boneless, lean pork |
| 3oz carrot |
| 6oz potato |
| ¼ onion |
| ¼ red bell pepper |
| 1tsp oil |
| ½ tsp paprika |
| ⅔ cup baked beans |
| ⅔ cup water |

1 Preheat the oven to 350°F. Rinse the pork under cold water, pat dry with paper toweling and carefully trim away any fat or gristle. Cut the pork into cubes.

2 Peel the carrot, potato and onion. Cut away the core and remove any seeds from the pepper. Put into a colander, rinse under cold water then chop into small pieces.

**TIP**
If using a food processor, drain off most of the liquid. Process then stir in the liquid until the desired texture is reached.

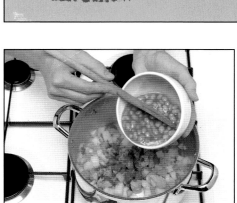

3 Heat the oil in a flameproof casserole, add the pork and sauté for a few minutes, stirring until browned. Add the vegetables, cook for 2 minutes then add the paprika, baked beans and water.

4 Bring to a boil, then cover and cook in the oven for 1¼ hours until the pork is tender.

5 Chop or process the mixture to the desired consistency, then spoon a little into a bowl. Test the temperature and cool if necessary, before serving.

6 Cover the remaining food and refrigerate as soon as possible. Use within 24 hours.

• Suitable for freezing.

# Chicken and Celery Supper

**Makes: 2½ cups**

| |
|---|
| 6oz chicken thighs, skinned and boned |
| ¼ onion |
| 8oz carrots |
| 3oz celery |
| 1 tsp oil |
| 2 tsp tomato or vegetable paste |
| 1 cup water |

**1** Rinse the chicken under cold water, pat dry, trim off any fat and cut into chunks.

**2** Peel, trim and rinse the vegetables and cut into dice.

**3** Heat the oil in a saucepan, add the chicken and onion and sauté for a few minutes, stirring until browned. Add the carrots, celery, paste and water. Bring to a boil, cover and simmer for 20 minutes until tender.

**4** Chop or process the mixture to the desired consistency. If using a food processor, process the solids first and then add the liquid a little at a time.

**5** Spoon a little into a bowl, test the temperature and cool if necessary, before serving.

**6** Cover the remaining food and refrigerate as soon as possible. Use within 24 hours.

- Suitable for freezing.

TIP
For extra flavor, add homemade broth instead of the water, or use a bouillon cube, but make sure it is low in sodium.

# Cauliflower and Broccoli with Cheese

**Makes: 2½ cups**

| |
|---|
| 6oz cauliflower |
| 6oz broccoli |
| 6oz potato |
| 1¼ cups formula |
| 3oz mild Cheddar cheese |

1 Rinse the vegetables, then break the cauliflower and broccoli into florets. Slice the tender stems but cut out and discard any woody core from the cauliflower. Peel and chop the potatoes into cubes.

2 Place the vegetables and formula in a saucepan, bring to a boil, cover and simmer for 12–15 minutes until quite tender.

3 Grate the cheese and add to the vegetables stirring until the cheese has melted.

4 Process or mash the mixture to the desired consistency, adding a little extra formula if necessary.

5 Spoon a little into a bowl, test the temperature and cool if necessary, before serving.

6 Cover the remaining food and refrigerate as soon as possible. Use within 24 hours.

• Suitable for freezing.

# Noodles with Broccoli and Ham

**Makes: 2½ cups**

4oz broccoli

2oz thinly sliced ham

2oz Cheddar cheese

1¼ cups formula

2oz noodles

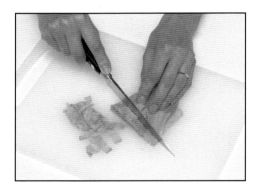

**1** Rinse the broccoli and cut into small florets, chopping the stalks. Chop the ham and grate the Cheddar cheese.

**2** Pour the formula into a saucepan, bring to a boil and add the noodles. Simmer, uncovered, for 5 minutes.

**3** Add the broccoli and cook for 10 minutes until tender.

TIP
Pasta swells on standing so you may need to thin the cooled leftover mixture with extra formula before reheating.

**4** Add the ham and cheese to the broccoli and noodles, stirring until the cheese has melted.

**5** Chop or process the mixture to the desired consistency and then spoon a little into a bowl. Test the temperature and cool if necessary, before serving.

**6** Cover the remaining food and refrigerate as soon as possible. Use within 24 hours.

● Suitable for freezing.

# Lentils and Vegetables

**Makes: 2½ cups**

¼ cup red lentils

¼ onion

½ tsp ground coriander

¼ tsp turmeric

1½ cups water

3oz potato

3oz carrot

3oz cauliflower

3oz green cabbage

1 Rinse the lentils under cold water, discarding any black bits.

2 Peel and chop the onion, then add to a saucepan with the lentils, spices and water. Bring to a boil, cover and simmer for 20 minutes.

3 Peel and chop the potato and carrot. Finely chop the cabbage and break the cauliflower into small florets.

4 Stir the vegetables into the pan. Cook for 12–15 minutes.

5 Chop or process to the desired consistency, adding a little extra boiled water if necessary.

6 Spoon a little into a bowl, test the temperature and cool if necessary, before serving.

7 Cover the remaining food and refrigerate as soon as possible. Use within 24 hours.

● Suitable for freezing.

# Fish and Potato Mash

**Makes: 1⅞ cups**

| |
|---|
| 8oz potato |
| 2oz leek |
| 2oz button mushrooms |
| 3oz frozen cod |
| 1 cup formula |
| 2oz Cheddar cheese, grated |

**1** Peel the potato, halve the leek and trim the mushrooms. Place all the vegetables in a colander and rinse well with cold water, drain, then chop the vegetables.

**2** Place the vegetables in a saucepan with the frozen fish and formula. Bring to a boil, cover and simmer for 15 minutes, until the fish is cooked and the potatoes are tender when pierced with a knife.

**3** Lift the fish out of pan with a slotted spoon and break into pieces with a knife and fork checking carefully for bones.

**4** Return the fish to the pan and stir in the grated cheese. Chop or process the mixture to give the desired consistency.

**5** Spoon a little into a bowl, test the temperature and cool if necessary, before serving.

**6** Cover the remaining food and refrigerate as soon as possible. Use within 24 hours.

● Suitable for freezing.

# Fish and Bell Pepper Rice

**Makes: 1⅞ cups**

| |
|---|
| 2oz celery |
| 2oz red bell pepper |
| 1¼ cups water |
| ¼ cup long grain rice |
| 2 tsp ketchup |
| 3oz frozen cod |

1 Trim the celery and discard the core and seeds from the pepper. Rinse and chop the vegetables.

2 Bring the water to a boil in a saucepan and add the vegetables, rice, ketchup and fish.

3 Bring back to a boil, then reduce heat, cover and simmer for 15 minutes, until the rice is tender and the fish is cooked.

4 Lift the fish out of the pan with a slotted spoon. Use a knife and fork to check for bones.

6 Spoon a little fish mixture into a small bowl, test the temperature and cool if necessary, before serving.

7 Cover the remaining food and refrigerate as soon as possible. Use within 24 hours.

• Suitable for freezing.

5 Stir the fish back into the pan and then chop or process.

# Chocolate Pudding

**Makes: 2**

| |
|---|
| 1 tsp cocoa |
| 1 tsp superfine sugar |
| ⅔ cup formula or milk |
| 1 egg |

**1** Preheat the oven to 350°F. Blend the cocoa and sugar with a little of the formula in a small bowl to make a smooth paste. Stir in the remaining formula and then pour the mixture into a saucepan.

**2** Bring just to a boil. Beat the egg in a bowl then gradually stir in the hot formula, mixing well to a smooth consistency.

**3** Strain the mixture into two ramekin dishes to remove any egg solids.

**4** Place the dishes in a roasting pan or shallow cake pan. Pour boiling water into the pan to come halfway up the sides of the dishes.

**5** Cook in the oven for 15–20 minutes or until the custard has set. Leave to cool.

**6** Refrigerate as soon as possible. Serve one pudding and use the second within 24 hours.

# Vanilla Custards

**Makes: 2**

| |
|---|
| 1 egg |
| 1 tsp superfine sugar |
| few drops vanilla extract |
| ⅔ cup formula or milk |

**1** Preheat the oven to 350°F. Using a fork, beat the egg, sugar and vanilla extract together in a bowl.

**2** Pour the formula into a small saucepan and heat until it is just to a boil.

**3** Gradually stir the formula into the egg mixture, whisking or beating until smooth.

**4** Strain into two ramekin dishes and place in a roasting pan. Add enough boiling water to come halfway up the sides of the dishes.

**5** Bake for 15–20 minutes or until the custard has set. Cool and serve as for **Chocolate Pudding**.

# Flavored Bread Sticks

**Makes: 36**

| |
|---|
| oil, for greasing |
| 5oz pizza dough mix |
| flour, for dusting |
| 1 tsp Marmite (yeast extract) |
| 1 egg yolk |

1 Brush two baking sheets with a little oil. Put the pizza mix in a bowl, add the quantity of water as directed on the package and mix to make a smooth dough.

2 Knead on a lightly floured surface for 5 minutes until smooth and elastic.

3 Roll out to a 9in square. Cut into 3 × ½in strips, twisting each to give a corkscrew effect. Arrange on the baking sheets, spaced slightly apart.

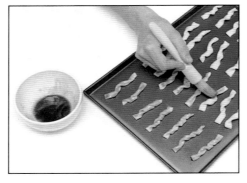

4 Mix the Marmite and egg yolk together and brush over the bread sticks. Loosely cover with oiled plastic wrap and leave in a warm place for 20–30 minutes to rise.

5 Meanwhile preheat the oven to 425°F. Bake the bread sticks for 8–10 minutes until well risen. Loosen but let cool on the baking sheet.

6 Serve one or two sticks. Store the rest in a plastic container for up to three days.

● Suitable for freezing up to three months in a plastic bag.

# French Toast

**Makes: 16**

| 2 slices bread |
| 1 egg |
| 2 tbsp formula or milk |

**1** Trim the crusts off the bread, then cut each slice in half.

**2** Beat the egg and milk in a shallow dish and dip the bread, one slice at a time, into the egg until coated on both sides.

**3** Heat a little butter and oil in a frying pan. Add the bread and fry until browned on both sides.

**4** Cool slightly, cut into fingers and serve as finger food or as part of a meal.

# Cheese Sticks

**Makes: 42**

oil, for greasing

1½ cups all-purpose flour

6 tbsp butter or margarine, cut into pieces

4oz Cheddar cheese, grated

1 egg, beaten

**1** Preheat the oven to 400°F. Brush two large baking sheets lightly with the oil.

**2** Place the flour in a bowl, add the butter or margarine and rub in until the mixture resembles fine breadcrumbs. Stir in the grated Cheddar cheese.

**3** Reserve 1 tbsp beaten egg and then stir the rest into the pastry mixture. Mix to a smooth dough, adding water if necessary.

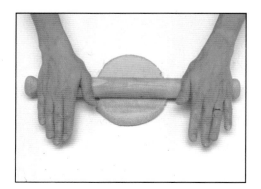

**4** Knead lightly and roll out on a floured surface to a 12 × 8in rectangle. Brush with the remaining egg.

**5** Cut the pastry into 3 × ½in strips and place on the baking sheets, spaced slightly apart.

**6** Bake the cheese sticks in the oven for 8–10 minutes until golden brown. Loosen but let cool on the baking sheets.

**7** Serve one or two sticks and store the rest in a plastic container for up to 1 week.

● Suitable for freezing up to three months in a plastic container, layered with wax paper.

TIP
Begin making these with mild cheese and as your child gets more adventurous change to stronger flavored cheese.

# Mini Cupcakes

**Makes: 26**

4 tbsp soft margarine

¼ cup superfine sugar

⅓ cup self-rising flour

1 egg

**1** Preheat the oven to 350°F. Separate 26 paper mini muffin cups and place on a large baking sheet, spaced slightly apart.

**2** Put all the ingredients for the cakes into a mixing bowl and beat together well until smooth.

**3** Divide the mixture among the cups and cook for 8–10 minutes until well risen and golden.

**4** Transfer the cakes to a wire rack and leave to cool completely, then peel the paper off one or two cakes and serve.

**5** Store the remaining cupcakes in a plastic container for up to three days.

● Suitable for freezing up to three months in a plastic container.

TIP
Cut a cupcake in half crosswise and spread one half with a little sugar-free jelly. Replace the top half and serve to baby.

# Sugar Cookie Shapes

**Makes: 60**

| |
|---|
| oil, for greasing |
| 1 cup all-purpose flour |
| 3 tbsp cornstarch |
| ¼ cup superfine sugar |
| ½ cup butter |
| extra superfine sugar, for sprinkling (optional) |

**1** Preheat the oven to 350°F. Brush two baking sheets with a little oil.

**2** Put the flour, cornstarch and sugar in a bowl. Cut the butter into pieces and rub into the flour until the mixture resembles fine breadcrumbs. Mold to a dough with your hands.

**3** Knead lightly and roll out on a floured surface to a ¼in thickness. Stamp out shapes with small cookie or petits fours cutters.

**4** Transfer to the baking sheets, sprinkle with extra sugar, if using, and cook for 10–12 minutes until pale golden. Loosen with a knife and let cool on the baking sheets, then transfer to a wire rack.

**5** Offer one or two shapes and store the rest in plastic containers for up to one week.

**TIP**
These cookies will keep well in the freezer for three months. Pack in rigid plastic containers and thaw in a single layer. If preferred, freeze the cookies before baking. Wrap well to prevent them taking up flavors from other food.

# STAGE 5: FROM BABY TO TODDLER

ONCE YOUR CHILD HAS REACHED 12 MONTHS HE OR SHE WILL BE ENJOYING A VARIED DIET AND VERY DEFINITE PERSONAL FOOD PREFERENCES WILL BE DEVELOPING. THIS IS ALSO A TIME WHEN FUSSY EATING HABITS MAY APPEAR. REMEMBER THAT A TODDLER'S APPETITE VARIES ENORMOUSLY AND YOU MAY FIND THAT HE OR SHE WILL EAT VERY WELL ONE DAY AND EAT HARDLY ANYTHING THE NEXT. BE GUIDED BY YOUR TODDLER AND TRY TO THINK IN TERMS OF WHAT THE CHILD HAS EATEN OVER SEVERAL DAYS RATHER THAN WORRYING ABOUT WHAT THEY DON'T EAT ON ONE DAY.

IN THIS SECTION YOU WILL FIND SOME FAVORITE BABY RECIPES FROM THE EARLIER STAGES UPDATED FOR YOUR GROWING TODDLER.

## FOODS TO INCLUDE

Give your child a selection of foods in the four main food groups daily:

**Breads, grains, and cereals:** include three to four helpings of the following food items per day – breakfast cereals, bread, pasta, potatoes, rice.

**Fruit and vegetables:** try to provide three or four helpings per day. Choose from fresh, canned, frozen or dried.

**Meat and/or alternatives:** one to two portions per day – meat – all kinds, including hamburgers and sausages, poultry, fish (fresh, canned or frozen), eggs (well-cooked), lentils and legumes (for example baked beans, red kidney beans, chickpeas), finely chopped nuts, smooth peanut butter and tofu.

**Dairy foods:** include 1 pint of milk per day or a mix of milk, cheese and yogurt. For a child who starts refusing milk, try flavoring it or using it in custards, ice cream, rice pudding or cheese sauce. A carton of yogurt or 1½oz of cheese have the same amount of calcium as about 7fl oz of whole milk.

Above: *Cereal and filler foods, like bread, pasta and rice.*

Above: *Fruit and vegetables, including frozen, dried and canned goods.*

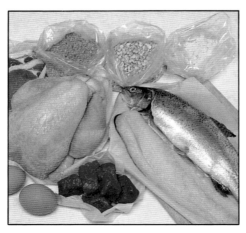

Above: *Meat and meat alternatives, like legumes and nuts.*

Above: *Dairy foods such as milk, cheese and yogurt.*

# Pasta with Ham and Vegetables

**Serves 2**

2oz small pasta

½ cup frozen mixed vegetables

2 tbsp margarine

2 tbsp all-purpose flour

⅔ cup milk

½ cup grated Colby or Cheddar
 cheese

2 slices ham, chopped

salt and pepper

**3** Stir two-thirds of the grated
cheese into the sauce and add the
drained pasta and vegetables, the
ham and a little salt and pepper.

**4** Spoon into two shallow dishes
and sprinkle with the remaining
cheese. Cool slightly if necessary.

TIP
This recipe also works well if you
use a 3½oz can tuna, drained, in
place of the ham. You could serve
the ham and vegetable sauce with
rice, if you prefer.

**1** Cook the pasta in a saucepan of
boiling water for 5 minutes.
Add vegetables and cook for 5 more
minutes until pasta is tender. Drain.

**2** Melt the margarine in a
medium-size pan and stir in the
flour. Gradually add the milk and
bring to a boil, stirring, until the
sauce is thickened and smooth.

# Shepherds' Pie

**Serves 2**

½ small onion

6oz lean ground beef

2 tsp all-purpose flour

2 tbsp ketchup

⅔ cup beef broth

pinch of mixed herbs

slice rutabaga, about 2oz

½ small parsnip, about 2oz

1 medium-sized potato, about 4oz

2 tsp milk

1 tbsp butter or margarine

½ carrot

3 tbsp frozen peas

salt and pepper (optional)

**1** Preheat oven to 375°F. Finely chop the onion and place in a small saucepan with the ground beef and sauté over low heat, stirring, until the ground beef is evenly browned.

**2** Add the flour, stirring, then add the ketchup, broth, mixed herbs and seasoning, if desired. Bring to a boil, cover and simmer gently for 30 minutes, stirring occasionally.

**3** Meanwhile, chop the rutabaga, parsnip and potato and cook for 20 minutes until tender. Drain.

**4** Mash with the milk and half of the butter or margarine.

**5** Spoon the beef mixture into two 1 cup ovenproof dishes. Place the mashed vegetables on top fluffing them up with a fork. Dot with butter or margarine.

**6** Place both the pies on a baking sheet and cook for about 25–30 minutes until browned on top and bubbling.

**7** Peel and thinly slice the carrot lengthwise. Stamp out shapes with small cookie cutters. Cook in a saucepan of boiling water with the peas for 5 minutes. Drain and serve with the shepherds' pies. Remember that baked pies are very hot when they come out of the oven. Always allow to cool slightly before serving to children.

# Lamb Stew

**Serves 2**

| |
|---|
| 4oz boneless lamb |
| ¼ small onion |
| 1 small carrot, about 2oz |
| ½ small parsnip, about 2oz |
| 1 small potato |
| 1 tsp oil |
| ⅔ cup beef broth |
| pinch of dried rosemary |
| salt and pepper (optional) |
| crusty bread, to serve |

1 Rinse the lamb under cold water and pat dry. Cut away any fat from the meat and cut into small cubes. Finely chop the onion, then dice the carrot and parsnip and cut the potato into slightly larger pieces.

2 Heat the oil in a medium-size saucepan, add the lamb and onion and brown. Add the carrot, parsnip and potato and sauté the lamb and vegetables for 3 minutes more, stirring frequently.

3 Add the broth, dried rosemary and a little salt and pepper, if desired. Bring to a boil, cover and simmer for 35–40 minutes or until the meat is tender and moist.

4 Spoon the stew into shallow bowls and cool slightly before serving with crusty bread.

# Fish and Cheese Pies

**Serves 2**

| |
|---|
| 1 medium-sized potato, about 5oz |
| 1oz green cabbage |
| 4oz cod fillets |
| 2 tbsp frozen corn |
| ⅔ cup milk |
| 1 tbsp butter or margarine |
| 1 tbsp all-purpose flour |
| ¼ cup grated Colby cheese |
| 1 tsp sesame seeds |
| carrots and snow peas, to serve |

**1** Peel and cut the potato into chunks and shred the cabbage. Cut any skin away from the fish fillets and rinse under cold water.

**2** Bring a saucepan of water to a boil, add the potato and cook for 10 minutes. Add the cabbage and cook for 5 minutes more until tender. Drain.

**3** Meanwhile place the fish fillets, the corn and all but 2 tsp of the milk in a second saucepan. Bring to a boil then cover the saucepan and simmer very gently for 8–10 minutes until the fish flakes easily when pressed with a knife.

**4** Strain the fish and corn, reserving the cooking liquid. Wash the pan then melt the butter or margarine in the pan. Stir in the flour then gradually add the reserved cooking liquid and bring to a boil, stirring until thickened and smooth.

**5** Add the fish and corn with half of the grated cheese. Spoon into two small ovenproof dishes.

**6** Mash the potato and cabbage with the remaining 2 tsp milk. Stir in half of the remaining cheese and spoon the mixture over the fish. Sprinkle with the sesame seeds and the remaining cheese.

**7** Cook under a preheated broiler until the topping is browned. Cool slightly before serving with vegetable fish.

# Broccoli and Cauliflower Bake

**Serves 2**

| |
|---|
| 1 egg |
| 3oz broccoli |
| 3oz cauliflower |
| 1 tbsp margarine |
| 1 tbsp all-purpose flour |
| ⅔ cup milk |
| ⅓ cup grated Colby cheese |
| ½ tomato |
| salt and pepper (optional) |

1 Put the egg in a small saucepan of cold water, bring to a boil and cook for about 10 minutes until the egg is hard-boiled.

2 Meanwhile cut the broccoli and cauliflower into florets and thinly slice the broccoli stalks. Cook in a saucepan of boiling water for about 8 minutes until just tender.

3 Drain the vegetables and dry the pan. Melt the margarine, stir in the flour then gradually mix in the milk and bring to a boil, stirring until thickened and smooth.

**TIP**
Making a face or fun pattern can be just enough to tempt a fussy eater to try something new.

4 Stir two-thirds of the cheese into the sauce together with a little seasoning, if desired. Reserve two of the broccoli florets and stir the remaining vegetables into the sauce.

5 Divide the mixture between two heat-resistant shallow dishes and sprinkle with the remaining cheese.

6 Place under a hot broiler until golden brown.

7 Make a face on each dish with broccoli florets for a nose, a halved tomato for a mouth and peeled and sliced hard-boiled egg for eyes. Cool slightly before serving.

# Eggy Bread Butterflies

**Serves 2**

| |
|---|
| 4 small broccoli florets |
| 8 peas |
| 1 small carrot |
| 1 slice Colby or Cheddar cheese |
| 2 slices ham |
| 2 slices bread |
| 1 egg |
| 2 tsp milk |
| 1 tsp light vegetable oil |
| a little ketchup |

1 Cook the broccoli florets and the peas in a saucepan of boiling water for 5 minutes. Drain well.

2 For each butterfly, cut four thin slices of carrot and cut into flower shapes with a small cookie cutter. Cut out four small squares from the cheese.

3 Cut four thin strips from the rest of the carrot for antennae. Roll up each piece of ham and arrange in the middle of two serving plates to make the two butterfly bodies.

4 Cut butterfly wings from the bread using a small knife.

**TIP**
Vary the ingredients for butterfly decorations. Make a body from a broiled breakfast sausage if preferred.

5 Beat together the egg and milk and dip the bread in to coat both sides thoroughly. Heat the oil in a medium-size skillet and fry the bread until golden on both sides.

6 Assemble the butterfly, using the eggy bread for the wings and decorating with the carrot, cheese, broccoli and peas. Use a blob of ketchup for the head.

# Pizza Clock

**Serves 3–4**

| 8in ready-made pizza base |
| 3 tbsp ketchup or pizza sauce |
| 2 tomatoes |
| ¾ cup grated cheese |
| pinch of dried marjoram |
| 1 green bell pepper |
| 1 large carrot |
| 1 thick slice ham |

**3** Meanwhile halve the pepper, cut away the core and seeds and stamp out the numbers 3, 6, 9 and 12 with small number cutters. Peel and thinly cut the carrot lengthwise and stamp out the numbers 1, 2, 4, 5, 7, 8, 10 and 11. Arrange on the pizza to form a clock face.

**4** Cut out a carrot circle. Cut two clock hands, each about 3in long from the ham. Arrange on the pizza with the round of carrot.

**5** Place the pizza clock on a serving plate and arrange the numbers around the edge. Cool the pizza clock slightly before cutting into wedges and serving.

**1** Preheat oven to 425°F. Place the pizza base on a baking sheet and spread with ketchup or pizza sauce. Chop the tomatoes and scatter over the pizza with the grated cheese and marjoram.

**2** Place directly on an oven shelf and bake for 12 minutes, until the cheese is bubbly. (Place a baking tray on the shelf below the pizza to catch any drips of cheese.)

TIP
If preferred, make a smaller version of this using half a toasted English muffin. Top as above and broil until the cheese melts. Add ham hands and small pieces of carrot to mark the numbers.

# Pancakes

**Serves 2–3**

| |
|---|
| ⅓ cup all-purpose flour |
| 1 egg |
| ⅔ cup milk |
| 1 tbsp light vegetable oil |
| *For the filling* |
| 1 banana |
| 1 orange |
| 2–3 scoops ice cream |
| a little maple syrup |

**1** Sift the flour into a bowl, add the egg and gradually whisk in the milk to form a smooth batter. Whisk in 1 tsp of the oil.

**2** To make the filling, slice the banana thinly or in chunks. Cut the peel away from the orange with a serrated knife, then cut the orange into segments.

**3** Heat a little of the remaining oil in medium-sized non-stick pan, pour off any excess oil and add 2 tbsp of the batter. Tilt the pan to evenly coat the pan and cook for a couple of minutes until the pancake is set and the underside is golden.

**4** Loosen the edges with a knife then toss the pancake or turn with a knife. Brown the other side and then slide out onto a plate. Fold in four and keep warm.

**5** Cook the rest of the batter in the same way until you have made 6 pancakes. Place two on each plate.

**6** Spoon a little fruit into each pancake and arrange on serving plates. Top with the remaining fruit, a scoop of ice cream and pour over a little maple syrup. Serve at once.

# Raspberry Sorbet

**Makes: 3¾ cups**

2 tsp powdered gelatin

2½ cups water

1¼ cups superfine sugar

1½lb raspberries, hulled

grated zest and juice of ½ lemon

**1** Put 2 tbsp water in a cup, sprinkle the gelatin over and set aside for a few minutes to soak.

**2** Place the water and sugar in a saucepan and heat, stirring occasionally until the sugar has completely dissolved.

**3** Bring to a boil and boil rapidly for 3 minutes. Remove from the heat, add the gelatin mixture to the syrup and stir until completely dissolved. Let cool.

**4** Blend or process the raspberries to a smooth purée then press through a strainer into the syrup. Stir in lemon zest and juice.

**5** Pour into a plastic container and freeze for 6–7 hours or until the mixture is half frozen.

**6** Beat the sorbet with a fork or transfer to a food processor and process until smooth. Return to the freezer and freeze until solid.

**7** Remove the sorbet from the freezer 10 minutes before serving to soften slightly, then scoop into dishes with a melon baller or small teaspoon.

**VARIATION**
**Summer Fruit Sorbet**
Follow the recipe up to Step 3. Put a 1¼lb package of frozen summer fruits into a second saucepan. Add 4 tbsp water, cover and cook for 5 minutes until soft, then purée and strain, add to the syrup and continue as above.

# INDEX

# ACKNOWLEDGEMENTS

The publishers would like to thank the following children and
adults for being such wonderful models: Maurice Bishop,
Andrew Brown, Penny and Chloe Brown, Daisy May Bryant,
April Cane, Helen and Matthew Coates, Cameron Gillis
Jamie Grant, Sandra and George Hadfield, Ted Howard,
Emily Johnson, Huw and Rhees Jones, Key, Stephen, Charlie
and Genevive Riddle, William Lewis, Sadé Walsh, Lionel and
Lucy Watson, Lily May Whitfield, Philippa Wish, James Wyatt.

**PICTURE CREDITS**
The publishers would like to thank the following for additional
images of babies used in the book:

Key: t = top; b = bottom; l = left; r = right.

Bubbles: pages 10 br (Jacqui Farrow); pages 21 t, 37, 67 tr (Lois
Joy Thurston); page 27 t (F Rombout); page 75 (S Price).
Lupe Cunha: pages 10 bl, 34/35, 40, 43 t, 56, 64, 73.
Greg Evans: page 80.
Sally and Richard Greenhill: page 62 t.
Lyons Waddell: page 59 t.
Reflections/Jennie Woodcock: pages 63 b, 66 tr, 76/77, 79, 87.
Timothy Woodcock: pages 10 t.